A SMALL PORCH

A SMALL PORCH

Sabbath Poems 2014 and 2015

TOGETHER WITH

The Presence of Nature in the Natural World

Wendell Berry

COUNTERPOINT

Library of Congress Cataloging-in-Publication Data is available.
ISBN 978-1-61902-616-2

Cover design by Kelly Winton
Text design by David Bullen

COUNTERPOINT
2560 Ninth Street, Suite 318
Berkeley, CA 94710
www.counterpointpress.com

Printed in the United States of America
Distributed by Publishers Group West

10 9 8 7 6 5 4 3 2 1

This book is dedicated, with thanks, to
Wes and Joan Jackson
David and Elsie Kline
Gene and Carol Logsdon

and to the memory of
Maury and Jeannine Telleen

Contents

PART III

The Presence of Nature in the Natural World:
A Long Conversation

A SMALL PORCH

PART I

Sabbaths 2014

I.

The long cold drives life inward
into shelter, into the body, into
limits of strength and time.

Out of darkness day comes.
The earth now white, the trees bear
bright new foliage of snow,

beautiful, yes. "Beautiful, but hell!"
Junior Wright said, wading
in knee-deep snow to feed

the snowbound cattle. We were young
then and really didn't mind.
This morning, half a century

later, under the beautiful trees,
beautiful truly, repaying much,
I dig out the paths again,

renewing again the pattern of home
life grown old in this place
and many times renewed. Continuing

my difficult study, I remind myself
again: "Take no thought for the morrow."

II.

TO THE NATIONAL SECURITY AGENCY

I am away in a quiet valley,
am busy at my quiet work
in this comely small cup of country
exactly fitted to my mind,
my mind to it exactly fitted.
It is enclosed by slopes and trees,
filled full of light and air and wind,
fulfilled by time and wear and weather.
My work is gathered of air and earth,
the history of the local light.
I am not going to tell you whether
or when I'm coming back. Don't wait.
Don't try to call. I have no phone.
There's not much left I want to shoot,
but I would like to shoot a drone.

III.

You don't know the day until
You've seen the last of it
Reddening the hill
And rising into night

IV.

Having carried them within her
five months, and labored hard
to set them free, the fierce old mother
finds her lambs, wet from her womb,
breathing the cold air, struggling
on the soiled bedding on the world's floor
to live, and she calls to them in loud
muttering gutturals of praise,
her absolute eloquence of joy, for they
who once were not, were nothing,
now are something, themselves, her own,
and her joy is at one with all joy
this world has known, and for the one
reason: The life that was not now is.

V.

The silence of the barn at evening,
when the shepherd draws shut the door
and starts home for the night, is heavenly,
for it says almost aloud that every lamb
is found, every ewe has found her lamb
and is feeding, and is content.

There is another of the barn's silences
that is heavenly also, for it says
that the ewes and their young ones now
are gone from it to new pasture,
the now-green, the first-grown grass
of the spring, and they are delighted,
the shepherd delighted with their delight.

VI.

The mockingbird sings
his praises of his mate
or of himself. In his joy
he knows no difference.

At first I called him silly
and egotistical, like all
lovers in the spring,
unable to say enough
of his ambiguous delight,
and so he repeats himself.

And then I said, "He's right!
Love teaches him to fail,
at this best of times,
to know whose song it is,
hers or his."

4/30/14

VII.

The old man from up the creek
and the hillside woods got sick.
In the loneliness of his misery
he discovered he did not care
whether he lived or died. What
a relief! Much encouraged,
he lives, wandering long times lost
to all who wonder where he is.

VIII.

A SMALL PORCH IN THE WOODS

Why do you force the knowledge of me to leave your memory and go abroad, you in whom my gifts proclaim me who have blessed you with the right bounteous gifts of so many favours; who, acting by an established covenant as the deputy of God, the creator, have from your earliest years established the appointed course of your life . . . . .

. . . . .

I am Nature who, by the gift of my condescension, have made you a sharer in my presence here and have deigned to bless you with my conversation.*

I.

Right-mindedness: a mind in place,
in right relation to Nature and
its neighbors. Thoughts, instructions,
stories, songs enter from outside, and some
of these are needed, can be made welcome,
but nothing replaces the living
geography, topography, ecology, history,
the mind's waking at home in its creaturely
household, which is its work, its burden,
its privilege, its intimate reference, its way
to find at need, against the time's perilous
leanings, the unshifting star.

---

* Alan of Lille (ca. 1116–1202 or 1203), *The Plaint of Nature*, translated by James J. Sheridan, Toronto, 1980, pp. 117, 126.

2.

In early April a heavy rain
such as never before in my time
scoured the Cane Run watershed,
gathering up everything loose
that the deepening runoff could carry
— mud (the soil!), logs, limbs, old leaves
and weeds, metal containers, bottles, shards
of plastic — the mixed mess left
in drifts on the bottomland pasture.
The land dried, made new and useless
to us by the cumber of the drift.
We picked it up, fourteen loads
of just the pieces big enough to obstruct
the mower, hauled it to the creek,
and threw it in — "If I've learned anything
from physics, it's how to throw things"* —
to be borne away on the ever-continuing
flow. This was the farm-making,
the lowdown work of the low lands,
never completed as Nature continues
serenely her world-making, in spite
of us if we oppose her, indifferently using us
if we would be her friends. And so
we are brought to her first law
that she, obeying, asks us to obey:
Keep the ground covered, taking *great pains*
. . . *to preserve the soil and to prevent*

* My grandson, Marshall Berry, who had finished his first year of college.

erosion.* Perennial vegetation kept
with care on the uplands and slopes
protects the soil, conserves the rain,
holds in place fertility and provision,
a kindness kept, a kindness given,
granting downstream an unstopping flow.
Good soil is a miracle, at once
holding and letting go. To keep so
kindly the land, the culture aspiring
to be high must cultivate the low
arts of land- and water-keeping.
Nature does not prefer humans
to the fish, the eagles, or the moles.
She *never did betray the heart*
that loved her † because she never did
give her preference to any heart,
loving or not. The truth is harder:
If we love ourselves, we have got
to love her. We must study
endlessly her long unending work,
thus learning to do our own, also unending,
making Nature our ally so far
as we can ask and she comply.
"It's good to have Nature working for you,"
said Henry Besuden, who knew.
"She works for a minimum wage."**

---

* Sir Albert Howard, *An Agricultural Testament*, Oxford University Press, 1940, p. 4.

† William Wordsworth, "Lines Composed a Few Miles Above Tintern Abbey."

** See my essay, "A Talent for Necessity," in *The Gift of Good Land*, North Point Press, 1981, p. 231.

3.

Old forest, tall household of the birds, no more
Will nimble deer browse as they did before
Deep in your peaceful shade, and your green mane
No more will gentle summer's sun and rain.

. . . .

All will be mute, Echo be still for good.
There will be a field where your great trees stood,
Their airy shadows shifting in the light. Now
You will feel the coulter and the plow.*

*

From Virginia, they came to wilderness
old past knowing, to them new. A quiet
resided here, into which came these
new ones, minds full of purpose, loud,
small, reductive, prone to disappointment.
They surveyed their places in it, established
possession: *Beginning on the bank*
of the Kentucky River at the mouth of Cane Run
at a hackberry . . . † Within that figment
geography of random landmarks,
the trees were felled. The plows scribed

---

* Pierre de Ronsard (1524–1585), "Lament for the Cutting of the Forest of Gastine," my translation, *A Part*, p. 61. Like Chaucer's and Spenser's, Ronsard's understanding of Nature was reverent, practical, and ecological, as is evident here. This understanding survived in English tradition as far as Pope ("Let Nature never be forgot"). The Romantics forgot the practical connection and the ecological measure.

† From an early "metes and bounds" deed in the history of the locality of these poems.

their lasting passages, exposing the ground
to the sky. The hot sun and hard rain
then came down upon it, undeflected
by a shadow or a leaf. What was here
that they so much wanted to change?
They wanted a farm, not a forest. From then
to now, no caring thought was given
to these slopes ever tending lower.
Thus Nature's gift, her wealth and ours, is borne
downstream, cluttering the bottomlands
in passing, and finally is lost at sea.

*

How with this rage shall beauty hold a plea,
Whose action is no stronger than a flower? *

8. Shakespeare, Sonnet 65.

4.

It is anno Domini 2014,
the year 239 of the newcomers
into Kentucky, the eightieth year
of the present witness, and now
along the wooded horizons we see
bare ruined tops of the ashes,
beautiful useful trees gone the way
of the landmark elms. This is the work
of the emerald ash borer, another
in the long succession of such articles
of trade — diseases, weeds, noxious
insects, birds, animals, fish —
in the centuries-old global economy:
the side effects, unforeseen
therefore unintended therefore
unknown to those best positioned
to profit by global trade therefore
debited inevitably to Nature, to the land,
to the land communities, unknown
as the future to those who take from them
every life and substance transmutable
to money, which fears no plague. And so
in our discounted woods our neighbors
the ash trees suddenly shine
as they die and the woodpeckers
remove the gray outer bark, and we
are poorer on our paltered globe.

5.

What was here that you wanted to change?
You changed at first your absence by your presence,
having arrived by a hard way over
the mountains or along the rivers. Once here,
your presence still was a sort of absence,
for you learned slowly and late where
you were. In ignorance, you destroyed
much that was here that you undervalued,
much of value that you never knew was here.

In ignorance, you have returned again
to absence from this place, this neighborhood
of the living and the dead where for a while
you almost were at home, its names and ways
that for a while were almost your mind.
What that was here have you given up
for your departure and your absence?
Or if you have stayed, going away
to work, what have you lost, forgetting
where you lay you down to sleep?
Or if you have stayed, driving over the fields
the great machines that have replaced
your neighbors and their work, their laughter
that gave to the work an ancient lightening,
a timeless grace, what have you lost?

.   .   .

Lost in old boundaries now merely
owned or rented at too great a price,
or lost in the dry maps of distances
away, set free of the once-new land
so much desired, so little known,
or tolled away by the old wish
to be as gods, or exiled by decree
of a powerful few against a weak "too many,"*
the people drift in scatters, homeless
as their garbage, on the currents
of a violent economy, their care and work
from their dismemoried country, beyond
every dreamed beginning, lost.

* Soon after World War II the official forces of academic agriculture and corporate industry
determined and declared that there were "too many farmers." This became government
intent, allowing the "free market" to discount and virtually destroy the small farmers and rural
communities. Too many country people concurred in their own disvaluation.

6.

A lookout upon a place to work,
live, move, and be in thought
of Nature's ancient precedence and rule,
a small porch from which to see the local
geography as a guide for thinking:

the valley like a cupped hand,
the compassing woods, below the woods
a two-track gravel road, below
the road a low-lying pasture bounded
by a row of trees along a creek,
the creek unseen in its deep slot until,
risen, it spreads upon the ground
the brought-down colors of the sky.

The road is an old way, made
by the wear of coming and going,
rutted by the outwash of storms
breaking across, kept by much
remaking, its life that of humans:
temporal and mortal. Even so,
how beautiful to see the bending
of its two tracks against the falls
and turnings of the slopes. The road divides

woodland and pasture, two ways
of making visible the shifts and passings
of the wind, two ways of giving
voice to the air, two realms of birds.
The invisible finds motion and voice
locally provided. Watch for its signs.

7.

The watcher comes, knowing the small
knowledge of his life in this body
in this place in this world. He comes
to a place of rest where he cannot
mistake himself as larger than he is,
the place of the gray flycatcher,
the yellow butterfly, the green dragonfly,
the white violet, the columbine,
where he cannot mistake himself
as more graced or graceful than he is.

At the woods' edge, the wild rose
is in bloom, beauty and consolation
always in excess of thought.

8.

The pattern for keeping this place
we must take from the woods, if
the land is to thrive in our using.*
If we were not here, Nature
would give this land to trees,
perennial, diverse, conserving
of land and water. The woods
is a great life of many lives
living upon its many deaths.
It flourishes in the dark crypts
of its decay. Seen from anywhere
inside, it is everywhere an unholding
enclosure of many columns,
roofed by the sky, containing
inexhaustibly itself. To the teachable
it is a teaching, not a syllabus
of processes and nomenclature
reduced to human understanding, but
the presence of the world being
made, a fabric of interdepending wonders,
moment by moment completed in beauty,
leaf shadows on light leaves moving.

* *An Agricultural Testament*, pp. 1–4.

9.

To care for what we know requires
care for what we don't, the world's lives
dark in the soil, dark in the dark.

Forbearance is the first care we give
to what we do not know. We live
by lives we don't intend, lives
that exceed our thoughts and needs, outlast
our designs, staying by passing through,
surviving again and again the risky passages
from ice to warmth, dark to light.

Rightness of scale is our second care:
the willingness to think and work
within the limits of our competence
to do no permanent wrong to anything
of permanent worth to the earth's life,
known or unknown, now or ever, never
destroying by knowledge, unknowingly,
what we do not know, so that the world
in its mystery, the known unknown world,
will live and thrive while we live.

.   .   .

And our competence to do no
permanent wrong to the land
is limited by the land's competence
to suffer our ignorance, our errors,
and — provided the scale
is right — to recover, to be made whole.

10.

The conversion of trees to wood to money,
which is all "the economy" asks,
is limitlessly the mistake of arrogance,
for it is the forest, not the tree,
that is the source of economic good:
the forest as the whole community
of itself, its lives living as the gifts
of lives lived. And so we come
to Troy Firth's precaution: Good forestry
is not predetermined by instruction
or methodology handed down by those
who presumably know to those
who presumably don't. It is, above all,
"observational."* Loving the forest,
you enter it to walk and watch.
As you observe its manifold and comely life,
it enters familiarly into imagination,
and so into sympathy. By sympathy
the mind in the forest is made at home.
From knowledge of the forest comes
at last knowledge of forestry:
what, without permanent damage,
can be spared and carefully removed,
leaving the forest whole. This learning
"takes decades. That's all there is to it."†

---

* "A Forest Conversation," in my essay collection *Our Only World*, Counterpoint, 2015, p. 48.
† "A Forest Conversation," p. 48.

II.

To sit or walk many days
and years, looking from the woods
into the woods, will lead beyond
methodology, beyond even sight,
into the sense, the presence, of the one
life of the forest composed
of uncountable lives in countless
years, each life coherent itself within
the coherence, the great composure,
of all. This no observer could make
or can explain. Within it, every
thought puts the earth at stake.

*

This great Grandmother of all creatures bred
Great Nature, euer young yet full of eld,
Still moouing, yet vnmoued from her sted;
Vnseene of any, yet of all beheld . . .

. . . .

To thee O greatest goddesse, onely great,
An humble suppliant loe, I lowely fly
Seeking for Right, which I of thee entreat;
Who Right to all dost deale indifferently...

. . . .

Sith of them all thou art the equall mother,
And knittest each to each, as brother vnto brother.*

* Edmund Spenser, *The Faerie Queene*, Book VII, Canto VII, stanza xiii, lines 1–4, and xiv, 1–4,
8–9.

12.

There is nothing random or by-chance (except
when "chance" signifies our ignorance)
in the forming of the woods. The effects
of hard weather, disease, human carelessness,
even these are caught up like dropped stitches,
gathered into the whole fabric, carried from
what was to what is to what will be. This is
the forest native to this place, its form
ever complete, never finished, grace beyond
all human comprehending. This is the form
of causes leading to effects that in turn
become causes, "the boundary of causation
always exceeding the boundary of consideration,"
as Wes Jackson puts it.* The form is shown
first by the shapes of leaves repeating,
like the chorus of a song. Trunk and branches
from the dark rise, divide, taper out and out,
each tree recalling a form never perfectly embodied
that yet is recognizable by kind among the mix
of kinds and their crisscrossings, each shaped
according to kind and company, place
and time, each by its story made among
the stories of the others. Each form is made
by reaching among shadows for light. It is shaped
by circumstances that its shaping changes.

* Often, in conversation.

13.

Explainers speak of the "stratification" of the forest: the tops of the tallest trees are "the canopy," then comes "the understory" of smaller trees, below those is "the shrub layer" of tallish woody bushes that are not trees, below those is "the herb layer" of ferns and flowers. Of all the strata above the ground the lowest is "the litter layer" of dead and decaying leaves, tree-fragments, fallen trees.*

These terms are useful, even true. And yet the forest does not stand still to be thus diagrammed. The tallest trees are found, at various ages, in every layer — to speak of one additional complexity. And yet all of the forest's parts, named or unnamed, known or unknown, are the forest.

We must include also the vagrant ferns, the fungi, mosses, lichens, vines, the creatures willfully mobile who crawl, walk, run, climb, glide, and fly, who pose to be pictured, described, and studied most readily when dead, whose needs and purposes, moods and motions all are contained, never extraneous or strange, within the ever-forming form.

* John Kricher / Gordon Morrison, *A Field Guide to Ecology of Eastern Forests*, The Peterson Field Guide Series, p. 7. (In fact, despite my quibble here, a pleasing, useful, recommendable book.)

14.

Birds people the heights, the low flyways,
the hidden passages among flowers and ferns.
And many times the watcher has imagined
what he may know but never see: the brooding vireo
in a thunderstorm at night, calmly roofing
her nest with her body and her wings while in
the dark the whole tree bends, the slender
branch stoops and swings, the hard rain falls.

15.

There is never an end to imagining
the lives of the birds. Or to wondering
at the superfluous beauty and unspeaking
flight of butterflies who light nearby:
the Eyed Brown, the Spicebush Swallowtail,
the Red Admiral, the Red-spotted Purple.
These so visible must stand for countless ones
and kinds easily overlooked or hard to see
or invisible. A world of words could not
describe this wordless world.

16.

The above-ground woods is confirmed,
sustained, immeasurably is made,
by the half or so of it that is underground.
We must acknowledge first that it is dark,
and we are blind by sight. This is the stratum
known only by result, where the dead become
alive, where the seed, abiding alone, dies
into the commonwealth of the living. We see
only by the light we bring, never to know
the dark lives as they are lived
in the dark. We mine out of this darkness,
according to our light, facts as dry
as bones. Can these facts live?

*

And in a launde, upon an hil of floures,
Was set this noble godesse Nature.
Of braunches were here halles and here boures
Iwrought after here cast and here mesure . . .

. . . .
Nature, the vicaire of the almyghty Lord . . . *

* Chaucer, *The Parliament of Fowles*, lines 302–05, 379.

17.

The woods is completed in beauty,
leaf shadows on light leaves moving
with the motions of the air.

So is the lowly pasture completed
in beauty, the bergamot, the milkweed
declaring themselves in season
among the ripened grass stems,
the grassblades, the blossoming clovers.

But are these beautiful because
we think them so, or because they are
beautiful in the mind of Nature
or the mind of God, beautiful
by intention inborn in a world beloved?

Beauty is the crisis of our knowing,
the signature of love indwelling
in all created things, called from nothing
by love, recognized and answered
by love in the human heart, not reducible
by any analysis to any fact.

The sufficient fact is unavailable.
The creatures came, as love imagines,
answering the loneliness of God
who needed them for company, as we
in our loneliness have needed them.

18.

Love is the crisis of our work.
When the watcher speaks of love
he is speaking not of history, not
of past or future, but of the love
in which all time has moved, in which
all things were and are and are to be,
the love that is before the beginning,
that is beyond the end, that is
entirely present as the flower of a day.

19.

Thus kan I forme and peynte a creature,
Whan that me list; who kan me countrefete?

. . . .

For He that is the formere principal
Hath maked me his vicaire general,
To forme and peynten erthely creaturis
Right as me list, and ech thyng in my cure is
Under the moone, that may wane and waxe;
And for my werk right no thyng wol I axe;
My lord and I been ful of oon accord
I made hire to the worshipe of my lord . . .*

*

Rising out of the crowd of lowly
foliage on the woods floor, a few
days in June, the white penstemon
risks the distinction of bloom.
At the top of the slender stem
the cluster of flowers appears,
not surprising for it is known
from other years, but as if suddenly
returned. Each tubular blossom,
pure white, five-lobed, opens
to reveal in its throat seven stripes
of most delicate purple, the middle stripe
the longest, with three shorter ones
symmetrically spaced on either side.

* Chaucer, *The Physician's Tale*, lines 11–13, 19–26.

For this, flower and watcher have not
waited or prepared, but merely lived
and the time of bloom has come.
For whose delight? The watcher gives
his sole certainty: "For mine." And what
depends upon this small culmination?
An ecologist of sorts, the watcher
does not know, but by its beauty
he is taught to answer: "Everything."

This is the Sabbath, the place, the rest,
from which we go to work. From here
the economies and politics of husbandry
are quietly attested in the heart.

20.

The forest serves the human economy merely by being a forest, giving to our use what we call its "products" and, if rightly used and spared, remaining a forest, intact, diversely living, after the gift is made. The pasture, like the forest, is Nature's gift, answerable to her laws. Like the well-kept woodland, the pasture, well-kept, covers and secures the soil, gentles and conserves the rain.

Unlike the forest, the pasture depends for its existence upon the farmer, his purpose, and his work. It is thus also a human artifact, maintained by grazing or mowing or both to interrupt the succession of plants by which the forest would return.

Because the farmer has made and kept it by his effort, his care for the grasses, clovers, weedy forages, and for the animals that live by grazing, his love for the pasture is unlike his love for the woods, but not greater.

*

The difference is made by his delight
in the delight, the fulfilled hunger,
of the good beasts of his choosing,
who depend on him, on whom
he depends. And all depends upon
a knowing, workday loving
to guide him in his work, in his watching.

21.

He wants to see the pasture green and thriving, satisfying the hunger of his sheep, who graze their fill, drink their fill at the creekside, and lie down in the shade to rest. In their rest rests the shepherd's soul.

The pasture joins its keepers to the world by ties, human and natural, more complex than they know, or will ever know. It keeps the harmony between economy and nature without which neither can thrive in human care.

It is economic by its yield of yearly life to the farm and its household. Subject only to human care and keeping, it is natural in its lasting, in its feeding of animals that feed people, in its living upon its own dying year after year, in its own community of creatures by humans uninvited.

The pasture joins its health
to the farmer's pleasure by the thriving
of his flock as it grazes among
the self-invited flowers,
by the nests the ground-nesting birds
have studiously placed and hidden,
by the covert nests and passages
of mice and voles, by the flights
of dragonflies, butterflies, fireflies,
by the delighted swallows flying.

22.

When the ground is safely kept,
when the scale is right, and when
the resident human mind
is righted by memory, affection,
neighborly kindness and care,
the giving of hands to work,
all lives of woodland and pasture
live by the economy of gifts,
the only economy that will last.
To be in one's right mind
is to know the right use of gifts.
To ask for more than is given,
to take more than is given back,
is to have less, and finally
nothing. This is not because
of any human wish. It follows
the law of Nature, mother
of all the creatures, maker
and giver of the native patterns
by which our world in changing
lasts, in dying lives.

*

Imposter, do not charge most innocent Nature,
As if she would her children should be riotous
With her abundance; she, good cateress,
Means her provision only to the good,
That live according to her sober laws
And holy dictate of spare Temperance.*

---

* John Milton, *Comus*, lines 762–67.

23.

Life does not relent or become
easier as death approaches
and troubles accumulate with age.
To pray to keep your mind as made
is as fearful as to pray to live,
for you may live into knowledge
worse than death. To forget
that some knowledge has been worse
than death is to be worse than dead.
How then may you come yet alive
to right-mindedness and right prayer?
Rightness of mind is only to be at home
in the place and the life you were given.
Rightness of prayer is only this:
Teach me thy love to know;
That this new light, which now I see,
*May both the work and workman show . . .**

* George Herbert, "Mattens."

24.

Almost lost in the mass
of neighboring foliage,
a plant clumsily named
Green-stemmed Joe-pye Weed
is singled out finally
by a cluster of pale blossoms.
It is not the most notable
of flowers, and yet once
an afternoon the sunlight
finds a way through
a hundred feet of leaves
and for a moment the shy
Green-stemmed Joy-pye Weed
receives that light and shines
in answer. Happy the man
who then is watching.

IX.

1.

The expert on resistance to torture
becomes an expert torturer.
The machine that helped a woman
to do her work replaces her at work.
The machine that helped a man to think
ticks on in absence of the man.
The communications technology that was
to become the concourse and meeting
of all the world, bringing the longed-for
peace to all the world, becomes
a weapon to break the world in pieces.

2.

Surely there is simple wrong, wrong
from the start, but the turning wrong
is worse: gains containing the seeds
of loss, amenities fated to do harm.
To warm our houses we set the world afire.
The gullible, the frivolous, the hard of heart
make of modern miracles normal
terror and perpetual war.
The first robot we heard of was a bomb.

3.

Will the robotic tree perform
the original miracle, transforming
light into life? Will the robotic leader
come at last to achieve our objective,
feed the hungry, forgive the debtors,
heal the sick, give sight to the blind,
release the captives, raise the dead?
Or do we look for another?

4.

If we surely knew that the man before us,
single in the multitude, would wreck
the plane that would wreck the tower,
whose fall would wreck a multitude
of living souls, who would not kill him?
If we knew for certain that the one man
in the cell would, if tortured, tell
the truth and save a multitude,
who would not torture him?

5.

After the mathematic of the Crucifixion,
who would not destroy one to save
a multitude, if by the destruction of one
so many reliably could be saved?
But that is as numbers are, and of us
who can foretell the future of numbers?
One small seed, lost in the multitude,
dying in the ground, sends into light
a mighty tree. But that is the original miracle
returned once again in time, and who of us
can foretell in time the future of a miracle?

6.

As the future is to fear, the ones gather
into the many who must be killed
unendingly, at endless expenditure
of death for life, of money for death,
of weapons for money. And the economy
grows unendingly, a faith to borrow
unendingly against, as the future is to fear.

7.

And we who walk in darkness,
the darkness we call our day, lighted
by the burning world, we need
the darkness for the foretold salvation:
We will save humanity by our willingness
to become inhuman. To save the world
we await the beneficent machine.

8.

O hasten, hasten through the dark
under the dim reminding stars
to find again what is small, tender, beloved,
the hope and mercy of this world
at the mercy of this world
in the darkest dark, the longest night.

9.

When our first grandchild came
to be with us, my father held back, unable
to bring himself again to give his heart
to another child, another who would
call forth his love, no matter the cost.
And then, knowing her smallness, her helplessness,
her inheritance of this world's sorrow,
he gave his heart, and so was given
what he had suffered longest and needed most.

PART II

Sabbaths 2015

I.

In the stiffened air the country hardens
into black and white, trees and snow.
Nothing moves but us warm-blooded ones
who walk and fly. In sky and river only
the living stir. My heart's fellow birds
come to the feeders for the seeds of their lives.
In our old world we live and wait
for the waters to flow, the winds to blow.

II.

You can divide a bird from its life,
your blade passing perfectly between.
But what you have then is not a life
and a bird. You have a dead bird
whose life now is nowhere you know.
After the passage of the blade, your study
of life has become the study of death.
Life cannot be stopped, its particles
divided and studied. Though life is
the part of a creature that causes it
to live, it seems in itself not a part
but rather a whole in which parts
of the world for a while participate.

III.

Nightmares of the age invade
my days and darken them,
but sometimes my sleep is lighted
by a better dream. One night,
as if in justice perhaps or mercy,
or by some kindness of this world,
I dreamed of my father. Long ago
he would play the piano, lively songs
of World War II, rocking on the bench,
sometimes singing, as he played.
And then a lasting sorrow came,
and no more piano music after that.
In my dream my father was again
playing the piano. He was beautiful.
He was smiling. He was playing
an elated improvisation on a tune
neither of us had known in the old time.
The notes shone singly as they gathered
brightly together. "Daddy," I said,
"you could play anywhere!" He smiled
at his thought's music, and played on.

IV.

We sleep and wake, wake
and sleep within the surrounding
sound of the falling rain,
hard at times, and the thunder,
all night long.

We don't need nearly so much
but so much is what we get,
no use complaining
or explaining: "It is climate change."
It is the climate.

The climate of this spring
will bring the woods' wildflowers
into bloom pretty much
together, glorious
all those old little ones
by the late cold and snow delayed,
by too much rain brought on,

who so far keep returning,
who have survived so far
the worst the climate can do,
and will this year survive
the present bad also.

. . .

What will be hurt by this
too much, and by in fact much less,
will be the naked fields,
thoughtlessly used, and then
absent from thought.

The earth thus regardlessly
is dispersed abroad, never
to return, not when
better thought may wish it back.

V.

They believe they've understood
belief in "the transcendent"
by disbelieving it.

Some mental feats remain
impossible even to the best
of human minds.

VI.

Now comes the overflow
not to be imagined but in time,
in season, in presence. This is
the splurge of beauty, transcending
every need we know. In her
greater knowing, great dame Nature
has called them, and they come,
the flowers in their thousands
under the still-bare trees, over
the dead leaves rising, moving
lightly as the air moves:
twinleaf, bloodroot, anemone,
violets purple and yellow and white,
bellwort. And the bluebells, whose perfume
cannot be recalled until
they are called back again. Who
would refuse this joy, this gift,
because in time it cannot last?

VII.

What a wonder I was
when I was young, as I learn
by the stern privilege
of being old: how regardlessly
I stepped the rough pathways
of the hillside woods,
treaded hardly thinking
the tumbled stairways
of the steep streams, and worked
unaching hard days
thoughtful only of the work,
the passing light, the heat, the cool
water I gladly drank.

VIII.

Love is a universe beyond
The daylight spending zone:
As one we more abound
Than two alone.

IX.

And now this holding
has held fifty-eight years,
a larger life we've lived in,
a welcoming room, a window
opening to the world.

5/29/15

X.

Patriotism blasts and crackles
all over the distant sky
while, blinking their silent code,
the fireflies rise out of the grass.

But wait. Call them "lightening bugs"
as we've always called them here.
Called by their right name,
they lighten our minds.

7/4/15

XI.

He sees by the light of the sun
and the sky's other lights
that come and go, revealing
at each return the changes
of the world, and the changes made
by humans of the world in time
for better or worse, some fearfully
for the worse. He sees also
by light given by teachers and friends
and the light that is left behind
in pictures, stories, and songs,
a staying light made
of the light's passing. As a further
wonder he has learned
to see by a light inborn
in himself, as in every leaf.
At last it has come to him
by being with him all along.
Of the world's one light, these
are the parcels he has gathered,
making a smaller light, his
by his willing to see by it.

To that light, itself invisible
were it not for the world
that is lighted by it, comes spring,
the circumstance of leaves,
the leaflight changing as the leaves

move, a motional language
of the invisible air, in which
also the colors of the flowers
declare the flowers amid
the crowding green leaves.
To see that these are wonders
he has only to wonder.
By loving them he sees
in them the signature
of the shaping love inwardly
moving them to bloom, as the air
moves them outwardly.

The machine that measures the light
does not see it. He sees
over the summer pasture
the dark swallowtails among
the beebalm's lavender flowers,
beauty far beyond
any purpose that he knows.
Beyond any hope
he could have had, he sees
among the shadows by the creek
the blue bellflowers suddenly
blooming on their frail towers.
The world lives by its beauty
in excess of need. In excess
of his absence, he is here
in the Sabbath beyond his reasons,
the Sabbath of measureless delight.

XII.

The old man is in the last days
of work he has done and loved
for many years. He is mowing
with his old team, the white horse
and the black, on the open hillside
under the open sky, within
the surrounding woods. This work
once was known by many
of his kind, and he is one
of the last to know it. But now
as his time grows scarce, his work
rarer by the day, its sights and motions
could be filmed, its sounds recorded,
it could be preserved perhaps forever
by wonders of modern technology.
He says no. He thinks no.
He refuses with his whole heart
the already futile wish to make
of a past present a future past.
Being so saved, his days
would be lost, would be no longer
even a memory. He needs these last
of his workdays. He needs them to be
his last, his own, such days
as do not come to one unwilling
to let them go. Had he been unwilling
for them to go, they would not yet

have come. Had he not been glad
to be the only one to know them,
he would never have known them.
If he remembers them to the last, giving
his thanks, how great will be his reward!

XIII.

The best of human work defers
always to the in-forming beauty
of Nature's work. But human work,
true to the nature of places
as it should be, is not natural
and is not a mirror held up
to nature. At best it is
the gift of the Heavenly Muse
to the farmer's art or the poet's,
by endless learning learned,
forever incomplete.

It is only the Christ-life,
the life undying, given,
received, again given,
that completes our work.

XIV.

1.

The creek in flood at night
is the auger that bores the hole
in time, through which we see
the making of the world, the water
loosed, floating the big rocks
beating them together, the rocks
beating the trees, the order
of the flow overcoming the order
of the staying ground, tearing it,
melting it, carrying it away.

2.

Our very fields are flowing,
earth burdening the waters.
To be made thus new,
the place must be made less.
And we who walk upon it
as it is being made
submit ourselves to making
by it as we have made it,
its history and ours made
day by day the same.

3.

How sweetly at other times
the flow declines, moving
silently from the riffle above
to the riffle below, the still
surface bearing fallen leaves
dry upon it, and as slow
as clouds in the bluest sky.

XV.

Again the air is full
of falling: the fall of the leaves
in the weighty season that brings
all home again to the lowly
miracle from which they came.

Nature, the mother and maker,
requires that life take form,
enflesh itself in the shapes
and habits of the world's unnumbered
kinds. And then she requires
each one at last to shed
its guise, giving up
its matter to the life to come.

Think of a world of no fall,
no gravity calling downward,
homeward, bringing all
by the light uprisen down
to rest in the resting land
— a world, instead, where all
that dies would fly upward
and outward, nameless and alone.
How sterile then would be
the earth, seasonless the year.

.   .   .

The year is the showing forth
of the heavenly love that is
the being of the present world.
The leaves, opening and at last
falling, hold a while
the beauty of God who made them
by the work and care of Nature,
His vicar and our mother.
His only is the light
of which all things are made,
the beauty that they are,
the delight that is our prayer.

XVI.

The year falls also from
the human-borne plagues
that kill the trees, foul
the air, the water, and the earth,
bringing to the world the curse
of frivolous death, the tiresome
novelty of wastefulness,
the ugly forethoughtfulness of fear.

What repair, what
return, will undo the consuming
self-belittlement that inherits,
disvalues, neglects, and ruins
the decent small farm —
the earned, kept, and cherished
good of a lifetime's work
gone — to break the heart?

And yet the light comes.
And yet the light is here.
Over the long shadows
the late light moves
in beauty through the living woods.

PART III

The Presence of Nature in the Natural World: A Long Conversation

The great trouble of our age, involving the whole human economy from agriculture to warfare, is in our relationship to the natural world — to what we call "nature" or even, still, "Nature" or "Mother Nature." The old usage persists even seriously, among at least some humans, no matter how "objectivity" weighs upon us. "Of all the pantheon," C. S. Lewis wrote, "Great Mother Nature has . . . been the hardest to kill."[1] With Nature we have, properly speaking, a relationship, for the responses go both ways: Nature is fully as capable of responding to us as we are of responding to her. In the age of industrialism, this relationship has been radically brought down to a pair of hopeless assumptions: that the natural world is passively subject either to unlimited pillage as a "natural resource," or to partial and selective protection as "the environment."

We seem to have forgotten that there might be, or that there ever were, mutually sustaining relationships between resident humans and their home places in the world of Nature. We seem to have no idea that the absence of such relationships, almost everywhere in our country and the world, might be the cause of our trouble. Our trouble nonetheless exists, is severe, and is getting worse. Instead of settled husbanders of cherished home places, we have become the willing parasites of any and every place, destroying the source and substance of our lives, as parasites invariably do.

This critical state of things has not always been explicitly the subject of my writing, but it has been constantly the circumstance in which I have written, for I have had constantly and consciously in sight the progressive decline of my home countryside and community. I have been perforce aware that this is a local manifestation of a decline that is now worldwide, affecting not only every place but also the oceans and the air, and I have of course felt a need to understand, and to oppose so far as I have been able, this downslope of all creation. In this effort of thought, I have been always in need of teachers, friends, and allies among the living and the dead. The mercy or the generosity accompanying this effort has been that I have found perhaps not all but many of the teachers, friends, and allies I have needed, often when I have needed them most.

By that I do not mean to suggest that my looking for help has been easy or carefree. To begin with, I never trusted, and after a while I rejected, the hope that many people have invested in what we might call the industrial formula: Science + Technology + Political Will = The Solution. This assumes that the science is adequate or soon will be, that the technology is adequate or soon will be, and therefore that the only essential task is to increase political pressure favoring the right science and the right technology.

An outstanding example of the industrial formula in action is the present campaign against global warming. If the scientific calculations and predictions about global warming are correct (which I am willing to assume that they are, though I have no science of my own by which to know), then its causes are waste and pollution. But "global warming" is a ravenously oversimplifying phrase that gobbles up and obscures all the myriad local instances of waste and pollution, for which local solutions will have to be worked out if waste and pollution are ever to be stopped. The phrase "global warming" suggests no such thing. Global warming, the language insists, is a *global* emergency: a global problem requiring a global solution. To solve it we have the science, we have the technology, and now we have only to prevail upon the world's politicians to enforce the recommended solution: burning less fossil fuel.

But from where I live and watch, I see the countryside and the country communities being wrecked by industrial violences: a heartless gigantism of scale and power, massive and irreparable soil erosion, pollution by toxic chemicals, ecological and social disintegration — and of course an immense burning of fossil fuels, making in turn an immense contribution, as alleged by scientists, to global warming.

. . .

I have no doubt at all that even if the global climate were getting better, our abuses of the land would still be the disaster most seriously threatening to the survival of humans and other creatures. Land abuse, I know, is pretty much a global phenomenon. But it is not happening in the whole world as climate change happens in the whole sky. It is happening, because it can happen, only locally, in small places, where the people who commit the abuses also live. And so my question has been, and continues to be, What can cause people to destroy the places where they live, the humans and other creatures who are their neighbors, and ultimately themselves? How can humans willingly turn against the earth, of which they are made, from which they live? To treat that as a scientific and technological or political question is not enough, is even misleading. The question immediately and at least is economic: What is wrong with the way we are keeping house, the way we make our living, the way we live? (What is wrong with our minds?) And to take the economic question seriously enough is right away to ask another that is also but not only economic: What is happening to our souls?

There is no industrial answer to such questions. Industrialism has never provided a standard by which such questions can be answered. I long ago hatched out of the egg in which I could believe that industrialism is capable of competent judgments of its effects, let alone competent solutions to the problems it has caused. Its "solutions," on the contrary, tend to increase the problems, as in the desperate example of industrial war, in which more never produces less; or the example, equally desperate, of agricultural pesticides, which must become more toxic and diverse as immunities develop among the pests. Since industry has no language with which to speak to us as living souls and children of Nature, but only as interchangeable employees, customers, or victims, by what language can we, in the fullness of our being, speak back to industrialism?

Seeing that my need for help was defined by that question, I have faced another difficulty: I am inescapably a product of "western" culture, first as I was born and grew up in it, and then as I, by my work, have made myself able to know it and more responsibly to inherit it. The difficulty was that western culture, especially when it is understood as Christian culture, however decayed, has been for many years in disfavor among writers and intellectuals, some of whom have seen it as the very origin of our unkindness toward "the environment." At its best, this disfavor has produced useful criticism, for professedly Christian institutions, nations, and armies have much cruelty and violence to answer for. At its worst, it is fashionably attitudinal and dismissive, so that we now have "Shakespeare scholars" who cannot recognize Shakespeare's frequent references to the Gospels.

For some, it has been possible and useful to turn away from the western or Christian inheritance to find instruction and sustenance in, mainly, oriental or tribal cultures. I am glad to acknowledge my own considerable indebtedness to the little I have managed to learn of oriental, American Indian, and other cultures, which have been often confirming and sometimes clarifying of the cultural lineage and faith that I consider my own. From Gary Snyder's Buddhism, for instance, I understood more clearly than from any other source that the practice of a religion is necessarily economic: how we live on and from the earth.

But I am too completely involved in western culture by the history of my mind, my people, and my place to be capable of a new start in another tradition. My need to make as much sense as I could of my history and experience, as I began fifty years ago to think of my task, clearly depended on my willingness to do so, not only as a native of a small patch of country in Henry County, Kentucky, but also as an heir and inevitably a legator of western culture. If I hoped to make sense, my culture would have to be always, at least implicitly, my subject, and I would have to be its critic. If I was troubled by our epidemic mistreatment of the natural or given world, especially in the economic landscapes that we live from, then I would have to search among the artifacts and records of my culture, in the time I had and so far as I was able, to find probable causes, appropriate standards, and possible corrections. This search began, as I would later realize, in my school years, before I could have explained, even to myself, my need and purpose.

Eventually, provoked by attacks on western culture as founded upon a supposedly biblical permission to humans to use the earth and its creatures in any way they might please, I read through the Bible to see how far it might support any such permission, or if, on the contrary, it might impose on humans the obligation to take good care of a world both given to them as a dwelling place, as to the others creatures, and to which they had been given as caretakers.

I found of course Genesis 1:28 ("Be fruitful and multiply, and replenish the earth, and subdue it: and have dominion over the fish of the sea, and over the fowl of the air, and over every living thing that moveth upon the earth"), which is the verse the detractors have found, and is pretty much the sum of their finding. But I also found that the Bible as a whole is a context that very sternly qualifies even the "dominion" given in Genesis 1:28. And I found many verses and passages that, even out of context, require humans to take the best possible care of the earth and its creatures. To speak to Genesis 1:28, for instance, there is the first verse of Psalm 24: "The earth is the Lord's, and the fullness thereof: the world and they that dwell therein." To that verse, singly and without context, if one takes it seriously, there are only two sane responses: 1) fear and trembling, and 2) a human economy that would conserve and revere the natural world on which it obviously depends. But it is possible for materialist environmentalists (as for many professing Christians) to read and not see, even to memorize a passage of language and not know what it says. It is easy, even intellectually permissible, to quote from a book that one has not read. And now most people are too distracted automotively and electronically to know what world they are in, let alone what the Bible might say about it.

In a world allegedly endangered by biblical religion, it is dangerous to be ignorant of the Bible. I must say, now, that I am not an uncritical reader of the Bible. There are parts of it that I dislike, but there are parts of it also in which I place my faith. From those parts, or some of them, I gather an old belief that God is not merely above this world, or behind it, but is *in* it, and it lives by sharing His life and breathing His breath. "If he gather unto himself his spirit and his breath," Elihu says to Job, "All flesh shall perish together, and man shall turn again unto dust." (Job 34:14–15) Like Psalm 24, these fearful verses clearly imply a mandate for the good care of all creation, and this becomes explicit in the Gospels' paramount moral commandment (Matthew 22:39) that we must love our neighbors as ourselves, even when our neighbors happen to be our enemies. This neighborly love cannot be a merely human transaction, for you cannot love your neighbor while you destroy the earth and its community of creatures on which you and your neighbor mutually depend.

The Bible, then, is not defined by misreading, or western culture by economic violence, any more than a body is defined by a disease.

Over the years, for my soul's sake and for the sake of my work, I have returned many times to the Bible, testing it and myself by such understanding, never enough, as I have been able to bring to it.

. . .

I have also returned repeatedly to the pages of several English poets, who lived and worked of course under the influence of the Bible, and whose interest in the natural world and the magisterial figure of Nature has been instructive and sustaining to me.

Both Chaucer and Spenser testify that "this noble goddesse Nature" or "great dame Nature" comes to them from a Latin allegory written in about the seventh decade of the twelfth century by Alanus De Insulis or Alan of Lille. This book, *De Planctu Naturae (On the Plaint of Nature)*, is composed of alternating chapters of verse and prose. It tells the story of Alan's dream-vision in which he converses with Nature, whom he recognizes both as his "kinswoman" and as the Vicar of God. The Latin original apparently is extremely hard to translate. According to James J. Sheridan, whose translation I have used,

> The author revels in every device of rhetoric. . . . He so interweaves the ordinary, etymological and technical signification of words that, when one extracts the meaning of many a section, one despairs of approximating a satisfactory translation.[2]

Despite its intricacy even in English, and the strangeness in our time of Alan's leisurely pleasure in rhetorical devices — he elaborates, for example, a sexual symbolism of grammar — this is a book extraordinarily useful to a reader interested in the history of our thought about the natural world as well as the history of conservation.

At the beginning of his book, Alan's happiness has been overcome by grief because of humanity's abandonment of Nature's laws. His own immediate complaint is against homosexuality, which seems to have been widespread and fairly openly practiced and acknowledged in his time. This he understands as a consequence that comes "when Venus wars with Venus."[3] For my own sake in my own time, I am sorry that he begins this way, for I am much troubled by our current politics of private life. Some of us now may reasonably object to Alan's view of homosexuality as unnatural, or anti-natural, but it would be a mistake to dismiss him on that account at the end of his first sentence.

As Alan continues the story of his vision, his objection to homosexuality becomes incidental to his, and Nature's, objection to lust, which is one of the whole set of sins that are opposed both to the integrity of Nature and to the integrity of human nature. The two Venuses that are at war are the Venus of lust or mere instinct and the Venus of responsible human love. This duality is analogous to, and dependent upon, the double nature of humankind. In the order of things, as in the Chain of Being, humans are placed between the angels and the animals. Strongly attracted in two conflicting directions, they have the hardship of a moral obligation to keep themselves in their rightful place.

Nature, then, as "faithful Vicar of heaven's prince," makes two requirements of us. She requires us to be natural in the general sense that, like other animals, we are born into physical embodiment, we reproduce, and we die. But she most sternly conditions her first requirement by requiring us also to be natural in the sense of being true to our specifically human nature. This means that we must practice the virtues — chastity, temperance, generosity, and humility, as they are named, their procession led by Hymenaeus,* in the *Plaint* — that

---

*Hymenaeus was once, until forsaken by her, the husband of Venus. The son of that marriage is Desire. In Alan's mythology, Hymenaeus is "closely related" to Nature and has "the honor of her right hand." He represents the sanctity, and the bad history, of marriage.

keeps us in our rightful place in the order of things. We must not be prompted by lust, avarice, arrogance, pride, envy, and the other sins, prodigality being the sum of them all, either to claim the prerogatives of gods or to lapse into bestiality and monstrosity. This is Nature's requirement because her own integrity and survival depend upon it, but she herself is unable to enforce it. She very properly acknowledges the limit of her power when she explains to Alan that although "man is born by my work, he is reborn by the power of God; through me he is called from non-being into being, through Him he is led from being into higher being."[4]

To put it another way: Humanity as an animal species —"the only extant species of the primate family Hominidae," says *The American Heritage Dictionary* — is a limitless category in which anything we may do can be explained, even justified, as "natural." But the necessity of our communal life as fellow humans, as well as our shared and inter-depending life as a species among species, imposes limits, defining, for the sake of our survival and that of the living world, a higher or moral human nature, specified by Nature herself in her conversation with Alan. The nature of every species is uniquely specific to itself. Human nature in its fullest sense is the most complex of all, for it involves standards and choices.

To speak of this from the perspective of our own time and the fashionable environmentalist prejudice against "anthropocentrism," it is our mandated human nature that allows us, by understanding the legitimacy of our own self-interest, or self-love as in Matthew 22:39, to understand the self-interest of other humans and other creatures. A human-centered and even a self-centered point of view is inevitable — What other point of view can a human have? — but by imagination, sympathy, and charity *only* are we able to recognize the actuality and necessity of other points of view.

It is impossible to speak of such things in a positivist or "objective" language, pruned of its upper branches and presided over by professional or specialist consciences embarrassed by faith, hope, and charity. And so it is a relief to resume the freedom and completeness of the language in which we can say that Nature, the Vicar of God, is the maker or materializer of a good world, as affirmed by Genesis 1:31, entrusted to the keeping of humans who must prove worthy of it by keeping true to their own, specifically human, nature, which is defined by that worthiness, which they must choose.

According to Alan's great instructor, the integrity of the natural world depends upon the maintenance by humans of *their* integrity by the practice of the virtues. The two integrities are interdependent. They cannot be separated and they must not be separately thought about. This is the moral framework of *The Plaint of Nature* and I would argue that it persists in a lineage of English poets from Chaucer to Pope, whether or not they can be shown to have read Alan. The same set of traditional assumptions can be shown also to support the work of a lineage of agricultural writers and scientists of about the last hundred years, as I will later demonstrate. So far as my reading, observation, and experience have informed me, I believe that Nature's imperative as set forth in the *Plaint* is correct, not just for the sake of morality or for the sake of Heaven, but in its conformity to the practical terms and demands of human life in the natural world. The high standards of Nature and of specifically human nature obviously will not be comforting to humans of the industrial age, among whom I certainly must include myself, and they are not in fashion, but that hardly proves them false.

.   .   .

As Alan grieves over the degeneracy of humankind, Nature appears to him. She is "a woman" whose hair shines with "a native luster surpassing the natural."[5] He proceeds to describe in patient detail her hair, her face, and her neck. He devotes seven fairly substantial paragraphs, in Sheridan's translation, to her crown, the jewels of which are elaborately allusive and symbolic. He describes with the same attention to detail and reference her dress, on which is depicted "a packed convention"[6] of all the birds; her mantle, which displays "in pictures . . . an account of the nature of aquatic animals,"[7] mainly fish; and her embroidered tunic, a part of which has been damaged by man's abuse of his reason, but on the remainder of which "a kind of magic picture makes the land animals come alive."[8] He discreetly refrains from looking at her shoe-tops and her undergarments, but is "inclined to think that a smiling picture made merry there in the realms of herbs and trees"[9] — which he then describes.

The presence of Nature is so numinous and exalted, of such "star-like beauty,"[10] that Alan faints and falls facedown. Though my interest is fully invested in this book, my own reaction here is much less excited, and I doubt that any reader now could find much excitement in this exhaustive portraiture, though I agree with C. S. Lewis that "the decorations do not completely obscure the note of delight."[11] The problem is that Alan's description of Nature is too distracted by his rhetorical extravagances to give us anything like a picture of her.

We get a better sense of her, I think, in his later invocation, in which he describes Nature's character rather than her appearance:

O child of God, mother of creation, bond of the universe and its stable link . . . you, who by your reins guide the universe, unite all things in a stable and harmonious bond and wed heaven to earth in a union of peace; who, working on the pure ideas of [Divine Wisdom], mould the species of all created things, clothing matter with form . . .[12]

It is no doubt wrong, or at least pointless, to ask Alan for a "realistic" portrait, as if he were dealing merely with a personification. His effort to describe Nature's appearance, exaggerated as it is, failing as it does, speaks nonetheless of his need to realize her, not merely as an allegorical person, but as a presence actually felt or known.

The really useful question, it seems to me, is not how Alan's Nature functions in a medieval allegory, but what she means historically as a figure very old and long-lasting, of whom people have needed, of whom some people need even now, to speak. How might one explain this need? My reading is sufficient only to assure me that Alan's vision of Nature draws upon a variety of sources, classical and Christian. She came to him as a figure of attested standing and power, he did imagine her, she did appear to him in something like a vision.

In Alan's *Plaint of Nature* and in Christian poems much later, the classical deities continue to appear, still needed by imagination, no longer perhaps as vital gods and goddesses, but at least as allegorical figures standing for their qualities or powers. That Nature takes her place prominently among them in the work of later poets appears to be owing largely to Alan. Sheridan says, "It is in Alan of Lille that she reaches full stature."[13] And according to Sheridan it was Alan who "theorized that God first created the world and then appointed Natura as His substitute and vice-regent . . . in particular to ensure that by like producing like all living creatures should increase and multiply . . ."[14]

And so Nature comes into the plot of Alan's Christian allegory reasonably enough, to keep company with Venus, Cupid, Genius, and a cast of personified vices and virtues. But if allegory tends toward simplification and a kind of shallowness — Truth is going to be purely true, and Greed purely greedy — Alan's representation of Nature tends in virtually the opposite direction: She is complex, vulnerable, mysterious, somewhat ghostly, less a personification than the presence, felt or intuited, of the natural world's artificer. She comes from an intuition of order and harmony in creation that is old and independent of empirical proofs. That we have personified her for so long testifies that we know her as an active, purposeful, and demanding force. Her domain, in the *Plaint* and elsewhere, is both natural and supernatural. As Vicar of God, she joins Heaven and Earth, resolving the duality of spirit and matter.

To say, as I just did, that we know her is obviously to raise the question of what we mean, and what we ever have meant, by saying that we "know." In our time an ideological tide has been carrying us toward a sort of apex at which none of us will claim to know anything that has not been proved and certified by scientists. But to read Alan of Lille is to realize that there was a time, a *long* time, when such knowledge was neither available nor wanted, but when many necessary things were nonetheless known. Thomas Carlyle, writing from his own perch in the modern world about the twelfth-century monk Jocelin of Brakelond, had to confront this very question: "Does it never give thee pause . . . that men then had a *soul*, not by hearsay alone, and as a figure of speech; but as a truth that they *knew* . . ."[15]

A century and a half later in the same darkening age, I asked my friend Maurice Telleen, who had much experience of livestock shows: "Does a good judge measure every individual by the breed standards, or does he go by intuition and use the breed standards to check himself?" In reply Maury said something remarkable: "He goes by intuition! A slow judge is always wrong." I thought his reply remarkable, of course, because it confirmed my belief that, among people still interested in the qualities of things, intuition still maintains its place and its standing as a way to know.

Intuition tells us, and has told us maybe as long as we have been human, that the nature of the world is a great being, the one being in which all other beings, living and not-living, are joined. And for a long time, in our tradition, we have called this being "Natura" or "Kind" or "Nature." And if we forget, our language remembers for us the relation of "natural" (by way of "kind") to "kindness" and "kin," and to "natal," "native," "nativity," and "nation." Moreover, as understood by Alan of Lille and the poets who descend from him, the being and the name of "Nature" also implicates the history of human responsibility toward the being of all things, and Nature's continuing requirement of that responsibility.

Contrast "Nature," then, with the merely clever poeticism "Gaia" used by some scientists to name the idea of the unity of earthly life, and perhaps to warm up and make congenial the term "biosphere." "Gaia" is the name of the Greek goddess of the earth, in whom no modern humans, let alone modern scientists, have even pretended to believe. Her name was used, no doubt, because, unlike "Nature," it had no familiar or traditional use, could attract no intuitive belief, or appeal at all to imagination.

.   .   .

By name Nature familiarly belongs to us, and she has so belonged to us for many hundreds of years, but considered from a viewpoint strictly biblical and doctrinal, she still may seem an intruder. Like the other classical deities, she joins the biblical tradition somewhat brazenly. The writers needed her perhaps because she has persisted in oral tradition, and because there remained not a Christian only but a general human need for her. That she usurps or threatens the roles of all three persons of the Trinity suggests that there was also a felt need for her to some degree in spite or because of them. Speaking only for myself, I will say that for me it has always been easy to be of two minds about the Trinity. The Father, the Son, and the Holy Spirit, as they appear in their places, as "characters" so to speak, in the Gospels, I have found simply recognizable or imaginable as such, but I think of them as members of "the Trinity" only deliberately and without so much interest. As an idea, the Trinity, the three-in-one, the three-part godhead, seems to me austerely abstract, complicated, and cold. The more it is explained, the less believable it becomes.

Perhaps it is this aloofness of the Trinity that calls into being and causes us to need this other, more lowly presence, holy yet familiar, matronly, practical, concerned, and eager to teach: Nature, the mother of creatures as the Virgin is the mother of God. And here I remember that Thomas Merton, in his prose poem, "Hagia Sophia," sees both Nature and the Virgin as sharing in the identity or person of Holy Wisdom: "There is in all visible things an invisible fecundity, a dimmed light, a meek namelessness, a hidden wholeness. This mysterious Unity and Integrity is Wisdom, the Mother of all, *Natura naturans*." And later: "*Natura* in Mary becomes pure Mother."[16] In Merton's treatment these three — Natura, Mary, Sophia — seem to fade into one another, shadowing forth an always evasive reality. And this, I think, is what we must expect when human thought reaches toward the mystery of the world's existence: an almost visible, almost palpable presence of a reality more accessible to poetry than to experiment, never fully to be revealed by any medium of human knowledge. And yet it is to be, it can be, learned and known, not by peering through a lens or by assemblies of data, but perhaps only by being quietly observant for a long time. Merton's vision does not explain or clarify Alan of Lille's, but between the two there is a sort of recognition and a mutual verification.

. . .

I am not entirely confident of my grasp of Alan's *Plaint of Nature*, partly because of my very reasonable doubt of my scholarship and understanding, but also because I am looking back at Alan from my knowledge of later writers who seem to be his successors, and from my own long preoccupation with the issues he addresses. For I do not, and I have not tried, to read Alan as a writer of historical or literary interest only. Despite the always considerable differences of times and languages, I have thought of him as a fellow writer with immediately useful intelligence of the world that is both his and mine.

His concept of the integrity of the natural world, and of the dependence of the world's integrity upon the integrity of human nature, leads by the most direct and simple logic to our own more scientific recognition of the integrity of ecosystems, the integrity ultimately of the ecosphere, and to the recognition (by not enough of us) of the necessity of an ecological ethic.

But a large part of the value of the *Plaint* is that, though I suppose it is as full as it could be of the biology and taxonomy of its time, it cannot be reduced to the sort of knowledge that we call scientific. It cannot, for that matter, be reduced to the sort of knowledge that we call poetic. It belongs instead to the great western family of writings that warn us against what we now call reductionism, but which traditionally we have called the deadly sin of pride or hubris: the wish to be "as gods," or the assumption that our small competence in dealing with small things implies or is equal to a great competence in dealing with great things. In our time we have ceased to feel the traditional fear of that equation, and we have a world of waste, pollution, and violence to show for it.

The Plaint of Nature cannot be comprehended within the bounds of any of our specialties, which exclude themselves by definition from dealing with one another. But once we acknowledge, once we permit our language to acknowledge, the immense miracle of the existence of this living world, in place of nothing, then we confront again that world and our existence in it, forever more mysterious than known. And then the air swarms with questions that are scientific, artistic, religious, and all of them insistently economic. Some of the questions are answerable, some are not. The summary questions are: What are our responsibilities? and What must we do? The connection of all questions to the human economy is finally not escapable. For our economy (how we live) cannot leave the world or any of its parts alone, as the ideal of the wilderness preserve seems to hope. We have only one choice: We must either care properly for all of it or continue our lethal damage to all of it.

That this is true we may be unable to know until we have understood how, and how severely, we have been penalized by the academic and professional divorces among the sciences and the arts. Division into specialties as a necessity or convenience of thought and work may be as old as civilization, but industrialism certainly has exaggerated it. We could hardly find a better illustration of this tendency than Shelley's "Defense of Poetry," in which he makes, with characteristic passion, a division between imagination and reason, assigning things eternal and spiritual to imagination, and things temporal and material to reason. *The Plaint of Nature*, as if in answer, resolves exactly that duality in the person of Nature herself, who joins Heaven and Earth, and whose discourse is of the vices that break her laws and her world, and of the virtues by which her laws would be obeyed, her rule restored, and her work made whole.

. . .

Nearly all of the *Plaint* occurs in Alan's dream vision, which is to say in his mind. It is an intensely mental work, if only because he worked so hard to render the style of it, and it becomes rather stuffy. Going from Alan to Chaucer is like stepping outdoors. Nature, the "noble emperesse" herself, is presented twice in Chaucer's work, once with acknowledgement of "Aleyn" and "the Pleynt of Kynde."[17] But in Chaucer, as never in Alan, the natural world itself is present also.

It has been said that in Chaucer nature is mainly idealized in dreams or paradisal visions. And I suppose it could be said that in his treatment especially of birds, he is a mere fabulist or a protocartoonist. But to me, his attitude toward the outdoor world seems in general to be familiar, affectionate, sympathetic, and, as only he could be, humorous. This we would know if he had written only the first twelve lines of *The Canterbury Tales*. A teacher required me to memorize those lines, and I did, more or less, sixty-some years ago. Since then I have found no other writing that conveys so immediately the *presence* (the freshness of the sight, feel, smell, and sound) of an early spring morning, as well as the writer's excitement and happiness at the thought of it.

Chaucer was a man of the city and the court, but I think he was not a "city person," as we now mean that phrase. London in Chaucer's time was comparatively a small city. Inundated as we are by the commotions of internal combustion, I doubt that we can easily imagine the quietness of fourteenth-century London, from any part of which, above or beyond the street noises, Chaucer probably could have heard the birds singing. Travel on horseback through the countryside was then an ordinary thing. This involved familiar relationships with horses, and on horseback at a comfortable gait anybody at all observant participates in the life of the roadside and the countryside with an intimacy impossible for a traveler in a motor vehicle. City people then would have had country knowledge as a matter of course. If they dreamed or imagined idealized landscapes, that may have been a "natural" result of their close knowledge of real ones.

And so in *The Parliament of Fowls* we have an ideal or visionary garden with real trees. And Chaucer's list of its trees is not just an inventory. He clearly enjoys sounding their names, but he also introduces them, so to speak, by their personalities: "The byldere ok, and ek the hardy asshe, / The piler elm,"[18] and so on. A little later he identifies the birds in the same way. *The Knight's Tale* also has its list of trees, but this one names the membership of a grove that has been cut down, "disinheriting" its further membership of gods, beasts, and birds, and leaving the ground "agast"[19] at the novelty of the sunlight falling upon it. Ronsard too felt this shock, this sympathy and dismay, at the exposure and vulnerability of the ground after the "butchery" of the Forest of Gastine (Elegy XXIV), and some of us are feeling it still at the sight of our own clear-cut forests. There is nothing fabulous or visionary about the Knight's small elegy for the fallen grove. It is informed by observation of such events, and by a real regret.

That the ground under the fallen grove was "agast" (aghast, shocked, terrified) at its new nakedness to the sunlight is not something that the Knight or Chaucer knew by any of the "objective facts" that industrial foresters would use to deny that such a thing is possible. The much older, long-enduring knowledge came from sympathy and compassion.

If Chaucer heard the birds singing in his own English, that was owing to his sympathy for them. Birds and animals use human speech by convention in literary fables, but that usage came into literature, I am sure, from the conversation of country people who lived, as some of them live still, in close daily association with the birds and animals of farmsteads and with those of the natural world. People who are in the habit of speaking to their nonhuman neighbors and collaborators are likely also to have the habit of translating into their own speech the languages and thoughts of those other creatures. There are practical reasons for this, and obviously it can be amusing, but it comes from sympathy, and in turn it increases sympathy.

Some years ago I wrote the introduction for a new printing of Theodora Stanwell-Fletcher's *Driftwood Valley*, a book I had loved since I was in the seventh or eighth grade. When I sent my typescript to the author, her strongest response was to my anticipation of the objection of some readers "to Mrs. Stanwell-Fletcher's anthropomorphizing of animal thoughts and feelings."[20] One of her degrees was in animal ecology; she was "scientific" enough to know that I was right. But her marginal note, as I remember, said: "How else could we understand them?" She spoke with authority, for she and her husband had spent three years in a remote part of British Columbia, where their nearest neighbors were the native plants and animals they had come to study.

From *The Nun's Priest's Tale* we know that Chaucer was a perfect master of the literary fable, but that tale signifies also that he was a close observer of the manners of household poultry, and he no doubt had listened with care to the conversation of country people — several of whom, after all, were in his company of Canterbury pilgrims. That his attention to them and their kind had been deliberate and lively we know from two of his portraits in *The Canterbury Tales*: those of the Plowman in the *General Prologue* and the "poor widow" of *The Nun's Priest's Tale*. The descriptions of those two characters give us a sort of compendium of agrarian values — that are, by no accident, agreeable to Nature's laws.

The Plowman is said to be one of Chaucer's "ideal characters," and I suppose he is, but his idealization does not make him in any way simple. His description, though brief, is ethically complex. The Plowman is an exemplary man and countryman because he is an exemplary Christian. He loves God best, and then he loves his neighbor as himself. He is a hard worker, good and true, and a man of peace. And those virtues enable his charity, for he will work without pay for those who need his help. If I am not mistaken, Chaucer's sense of humor is at work here, pointed at those who think of goodness as a sacrifice paid here for admission to Heaven. The Plowman's virtues are understood as solidly practical and economic. He is a good neighbor, and good neighbors are likely to *have* good neighbors. The payoff, to complete the joke, may be Heavenly, but it is also earthly: A good neighborhood is an economic asset to all of its members.

The portrait of the elderly widow in *The Nun's Priest's Tale* attends to other practical and necessary virtues: patience, frugality, and good husbandry. These are congenial with the virtues of the Plowman and complete them, as his virtues complete hers. That the whole set of virtues is divided between the two characters is a matter only of appropriateness. The widow lives with her two daughters in a small cottage. She owns (God has "sente"[21] her) three large sows, three cows, a sheep named Malle (Mollie?), seven hens, and a rooster. She works "out" as a "dairymaid," but it is clear that her economy is most securely founded upon her own small holding and her few head of livestock, also upon needing little. She needs no "poignant sauce"[22] for her food because the food is good and hunger seasons it well. Her charity is to need no charity, another recognized way of being a good neighbor in a country community. This widow is a first cousin to the old Corycian farmer in Virgil's fourth Georgic. She practices exactly the "cottage economy" later praised and advocated by William Cobbett (and others).

. . .

My approach to Chaucer's first representation of Nature has been backwards, from late work to early, as a way of knowing how he understood her. If we read *The Parliament of Fowls* simply as an exemplary "dream-vision" by a master poet and courtier, then perhaps we are free to regard the figure of Nature as a pleasing, even a beautiful, "picture" borrowed from Alan's *Plaint* and requiring little more of us than to place the poem historically and to appreciate it critically. But if we would like to take seriously this appearance or apparition of Nature, then we have to ask how seriously Chaucer took it, and that is not so easy. It helps, I think, if we conceive of Chaucer not only as the great poet and sophisticated "man of the world" that he certainly was, but also, and on the evidence of his writing, a man on easy speaking terms with the countryside and all of its inhabitants.

The poem is a dream-vision, a lighthearted fantasy, above all a comedy. It also takes place in an actual landscape, in which the poet is well-acquainted with the trees, the flowers, and the birds. The birds speak English, sometimes at length, but they speak also in their own tongues. We hear from the goose, the cuckoo, and the duck all together and all in the same line: "Kek kek! kokkow! quek quek!"[23] When they speak English, they use images that might have been used at court or by a farmer's hearth, but they certainly came from people who had spent time outdoors at night: "There are more stars, God knows, than a pair" and "You fare by love as owls do by light."[24]

Faced with the possibility of copying Alan's vision of Nature in her extremely elaborate finery, Chaucer politely declines by referring us to the *Plaint*, where we can find her in "such array."[25] This is a part of the comedy, but it leaves him free to describe her in his own way, which he does by a single graceful compliment which serves to acknowledge her sanctity and her standing: She is so far fairer "than any creature"[26] as the summer sun's light surpasses that of any star. And then, it seems, he draws aside a curtain:

She is sitting in a forest glade on a flowery hill. She is "set off" by halls and bowers of branches — evergreen branches, as Chaucer's readers must always have assumed — that have been "wrought"[27] according to her design. This is Nature in her English vicarage. She sits before us as a distinctly hieratic figure, yet made familiar by the homely setting that combines art and nature. This is clearly akin to the scene in which, two and a half centuries later, Robert Herrick's Corinna will go a-Maying:

> Come, my Corinna, come; and comming, marke
> How each field turns a street; each street a Parke
>> Made green, and trimm'd with trees: see how
>> Devotion gives each House a Bough,
>> Or Branch: Each Porch, each doore, ere this,
>> An arke a Tabernacle is
> Made up of white-thorn neatly enterwove . . .[28]

Chaucer's "noble emperesse, ful of grace"[29] seems perfectly to belong here, in the center of such a mating ritual as he must have witnessed many times. She is there, not in May but on Saint Valentine's day, as in every year, to see to the matchmaking of all the birds, according to her judgment. To see that they in their great numbers find mates and reproduce after their kinds is her high office. Following Alan's doctrine, Chaucer has her presiding as

>> the vicaire of the almyghty Lord,
>> That hot, cold, hevy, light, moyst, and dreye
>> Hath knyt by evene noumbres of acord . . .[30]

Her work is to reconcile the world's opposites and contentions into a lasting, self-renewing composure.

From Nature enthroned our attention is drawn to the assembly of all the birds, to the clamorous low "common sense" of the goose, the cuckoo, and the duck, and finally to the elegant "roundel" that the mated birds all sing together at the end. These incongruities take nothing away from Nature's dignity and they don't need to be justified or explained. They notify us of the range of Chaucer's art and his knowledge, authenticated by the world itself, which often puts high seriousness and low comedy into the same event or the same instant.

But let us go ahead and ask the modern question: Did Chaucer "believe in" this Nature? Did he "know" her? Did he "actually see" her seated in her glade "upon an hil of floures"? Well, he seems to have seen her there, he seems to have invited me to see her, and I too seem to have seen her. Where are the proofs? There are of course no proofs, no photograph, no second witness. But we are talking here about the imaginative life of a country — not a nation, a *country* — which, in its apprehension of the natural world and its "invisible fecundity," its "hidden wholeness," always must outreach its proofs, its sciences, its mechanic arts, its political economy, its market. If it fails in that, as it has with us, then we get probably what we have got: a country, mainly unknown to its occupying humans, rapidly melting into a toxic slurry and flowing away through its rivers.

That Alan's Nature appears again, years later, in the *Canterbury Tales* suggests that Chaucer thought her important enough to keep her in mind to the end of his life. At the beginning of his tale, the Physician "quotes" what he imagines she would say of the singular beauty of Virginia, his chaste heroine. Though the Physician is a man whose honesty needs watching, we need not doubt his characterization of Nature. Following his professional habit of learned speech, he has Nature describe herself in keeping with Alan's description, and with Chaucer's in *The Parliament of Fowls*. She is God's "vicar general,"[31] in charge of the sublunar creation, whose "forming and painting"[32] of the creatures is work done "to the worship of my lord."[33] What may be unique here is her insistence that her work cannot be "counterfeited."[34] In this, she takes the side of William Carlos Williams* and others in our own time,

---

* In especially some of the most lucid prose passage of *Spring and All*.

against Hamlet et al. who have argued that the "end" of art "was and is to hold . . . the mirror up to Nature . . ."[35]

This disagreement is of interest now because it clearly defines the problem confronted by scientists of the last hundred or so years who have, against the industrial declivity, taken an ecological approach to our use of the land, primarily in agriculture. To those scientists, whose work I will discuss later in this essay, two truths have been obvious: first, that we humans cannot live in unaltered natural settings, for we passed up our chance to be "rational apes" too long ago; and, second, though we cannot make mirror images of natural places, even if we could do so, even if we could live in them if we could make them, we nonetheless are obliged to obey Nature's laws, which are imposed absolutely and will never change.

.   .   .

From Alan's vision of Nature, and then from Chaucer's, came Spencer's (as he testifies) in the fragmentary seventh book of *The Faerie Queene*, and of these three Spenser's is the finest. It is the most fully developed and detailed and the richest in meaning. The story he places Nature in, as he tells it, is the most dramatic. And the problem he sets for her is one that was urgent for him then, and that seems still more urgent for us.

Book VII of *The Faerie Queene* contains only the sixth and seventh cantos and two stanzas of an eighth. These are known as "the Mutability cantos," for they tell how "the Titanesse," Mutability, rebels against the classical deities and attempts to establish her sovereignty over them, and over all creation. She disdains the rule of Jove, and refuses to accept his judgment, appealing instead to "the highest him . . . Father of Gods and men . . . the God of Nature."[36] And so great Nature herself, as God's deputy, comes to preside over a trial to determine the justice of Mutability's claim. For this all the creatures are assembled on Arlo hill, where they are "well disposed" by Order, who is "Natures Sergeant."[37]

And then Nature enters with the great processional dignity that Spenser seems to have learned from the twenty-fourth Psalm,* as maybe of all poets only he could have learned from it:

> Then forth issewed (great goddesse) great dame *Nature*,
>> With goodly port and gracious Maiesty;
>> Being far greater and more tall of stature
>> Then any of the gods or Powers on hie:
>> Yet certes by her face and physnomy,
>> Whether she man or woman inly were,
>> That could not any creature well descry:
>> For, with a veile that wimpled euery where,
> Her head and face was hid, that mote to none appeare.
>
> That some doe say was so by skill deuized,
>> To hide the terror of her vncouth hew,
>> From mortall eyes that should be sore agrized;
>> That eye of wight could not indure to view:
>> But others tell that it so beautious was,
>> And round about such beames of splendor threw,
>> That it the Sunne a thousand times did pass,
> Ne could be seene, but like an image in a glass.
>
> That well may seemen true: for, well I weene
>> That this same day, when she on *Arlo* sat,
>> Her garment was so bright and wondrous sheene,
>> That my fraile wit cannot deuize to what

---

* This assumption is fairly obvious if one is thinking also of the twelfth stanza of his "Epithalamion." Only a poet of the greatest skill, and confidence, would have attempted this.

It to compare, nor finde like stuffe to that,
    As those three sacred *Saints*, though else most wise,
    Yet on mount *Thabor* quite their wits forgat,
    When they their glorious Lord in strange disguise
Transfigur'd sawe; his garments so did daze their eyes.

· ·

This great Grandmother of all creatures bred
    Great *Nature*, euer young yet full of eld,
    Still moouing, yet vnmoued from her sted;
    Vnseene of any, yet of all beheld . . .[38]

This representation of Nature clearly derives from those of Alan of Lille and Chaucer, but the resemblance, though unmistakable, is distant. Here there is nothing at all of Alan's relentless accumulation of details. And in our own time, when poets are supposed or expected to disown their forebears, it is a relief to come upon Spenser's filial devotion to Chaucer, but nothing here reminds us of the at-home conviviality of Nature's presidence over the Parliament of Fowls.

Spenser's Nature is altogether hieratic and luminous. In a way that recalls Dante's frustration in the *Paradiso*, Spenser describes this "great goddesse" mostly by describing his inability to describe her. Though she is heavily veiled like perhaps a nun and he refers to her always by feminine pronouns, she may be "inly" either a man or a woman, and her face is either unendurably terrible or so radiantly beautiful that it could not be seen except "through a glass darkly." And in describing her, Spenser, unlike Alan and Chaucer, recalls the Gospels, for her garment was "so bright and wondrous sheene" as to recall the garments of Christ at the Transfiguration. And here Spenser must be remembering also the Gospel of John 1:3: "All things were made by him; and without him was not any thing made that was made."

Furthermore, Mutability, in pleading her case before Nature, addresses her as "greatest goddesse, only great"

> Who Right to all dost deale indifferently,
> Damning all Wrong and tortuous Iniurie,
> Which any of thy creatures doe to other
> (Oppressing them with power, vnequally)
> Sith of them all thou art the equall mother,
> And knittest each to each, as brother vnto brother.[39]

Any twenty-first-century reader familiar with the formal principle of interdependence, as it operates in ecosystems, will recognize this "knitting" for what it is and means, as they will recognize also Nature's "equal" motherhood of "all" the creatures. Her "indifference" is not apathetic; she is merely impartial, preferring no single species over any other, just as the realists of present-day biology know her to be. And this supposedly modern perception is much older than Spenser, for he took it from the *Plaint* in which, four hundred years earlier, Nature had warned Alan that "my bounteous power does not shine forth in you alone individually but also universally in all things."[40] We have our lives by no right of our own, but instead by the privilege of sharing in the life that sustains all creatures. This great convocation is the work of Nature, its "equall mother," which makes her not only, as Alan saw, our teacher, but also, as Spenser was first to see, our judge.

And so, submitting to Nature as the supreme worldly authority, Mutability presents her argument, and summons a procession of witnesses: the earth, the four elements, the seasons, the months, day and night, and finally life and death, all of whom support her argument. Jove then argues that worldly change is ruled by the "heavenly" gods. But Mutability charges and proves the changingness of the planetary deities, of the sun, which is sometimes eclipsed, and of Jove himself, who once was not and then was born. She is an unbluffable, brilliant lawyer, and her case is nearly perfect, as is the poetry that Spenser gives to it.

Finally, after a long considering pause, Nature gives her verdict:

> I well consider all that ye haue sayd,
>> And find that all things stedfastnes doe hate
>> And changed be: yet being rightly wayd
>> They are not changed from their first estate;
>> But by their change their being doe dilate:
>> And turning to themselues at length againe,
>> Doe worke their owne perfection so by fate:
>> Then ouer them Change doth not rule and raigne;
> But they raigne ouer change, and doe their states maintaine.[41]

C. S. Lewis speaks, with justice, of the "deep obscurity"[42] of those lines. But we may clarify them somewhat by placing beside them these earlier lines in which Mutability argues that

> For, all that from [Earth] springs, and is ybredde,
>> How-euer fayre it flourish for a time,
>> Yet see we soone decay; and, being dead,
>> To turne again vnto their earthly slime:
>> Yet, out of their decay and mortall crime,
>> We daily see new creatures to arize;
>> And of their Winter spring another Prime,
>> Vnlike in forme, and chang'd by strange disguise . . .[43]

Mutability here seems to argue, rather craftily, that change is absolute, leading invariably to something "unlike" and entirely new. Nature, if at the end she is remembering those lines, sees them as an imperfect

description of a natural cycle capable of endlessly repeating itself —
with, we would now say, occasional variations or "mutations," and
depending on appropriate human cooperation. In her verdict, Nature
readily acknowledges the ceaselessness of change, but she confirms, if
not quite clearly, its cyclicality as greater, and as a form, or *the* form, of
stability. She would have been confirmed in this by the *Plaint* where,
in Alan's vision of her, Nature says (more clearly) that

> it was God's will that by a mutually related circle of birth and death,
> transitory things should be given stability by instability, endlessness
> by endings, eternity by temporariness, and that the series of things
> should ever be knit by successive renewals of birth.[44]

This will be better understood about three and a half centuries later by
scientists aware of the biology, and the supreme economic importance,
of the fertility cycle.

At the end of Canto VII, Nature, having completed her work for
the time being, "did vanish, whither no man wist."[45] *The Faerie Queene*,
as we have it, ends two stanzas later with Spenser's prayer for the
"Sabaoths sight"

> Of that same time when no more *Change* shall be,
> But stedfast rest of all things firmely stayd
> Vpon the pillours of Eternity . . .[46]

Nature's standing in the order of things, as Spenser understood it, is
exalted, well above that of humanity, and she has about her the nim-
bus of sanctity. Her equitable motherhood of all the creatures and
her judgeship over them impose upon humans a responsibility that
is both worshipful and relentlessly practical. But the order in which
she is placed is firmly Christian, and her jurisdiction is limited to the

incarnate world. Reassuring as may be her verdict against Mutability, it offers little comfort to individual humans in their suffering of their own mortality and that of their loved ones. And so *The Faerie Queene* as we have it, though incomplete, ends appropriately by invoking our so far undying hope for a "time," beyond Nature's world and all of its stories, "when no more change shall be."

Within the compass of my reading, Spenser's vision of Nature is the highest and fullest, the most responsibly imagined, the most complete, and the most instructive. And this, I think, is because it is the most thoughtful. In the Mutability cantos, Spenser confronts a question serious enough to have no definitive or final answer: On what terms are we to live with the perpetual changingness of this world? And he answers with an argument meticulously constructed. That his stanzas on Nature's appearance are so complex and beautiful must be partly the result of his thoughtfulness. I do not mean that he used his poetry as a vehicle to express or communicate his finished thought, but rather that his poetry was the vital means by which his thinking was done. Strange as it may seem to say this after the division of the mental functions into departments, it is clear that some poets have recognized that poetry in its way, like prose in its way, can be serviceable to thought, and when they have needed to do so they have used it as a way to think.

. . .

After Spenser, so far as I have read or remember, no other English poet acknowledged the influence of Alan of Lille or thought so carefully about Nature — probably because, after Spenser, no poet needed to think so carefully about her. But there certainly have been other English poets who appear to have been influenced by the earlier visions of Nature, and who have contributed to a line of thought about the proper human use of the natural world.

Passages in the eleventh and twelfth parts of *Piers Plowman* suggest that William Langland, for one, had read *The Plaint of Nature*. C. S. Lewis assumed that he had.[47] A remarkable difference is that, to Langland, Nature or "Kynde," rather than the vicar of God, is God Himself. Langland, anyhow, was a better naturalist than either Chaucer or Spenser. Kynde instructs him in a dream to study the creatures, "the wonders of this world," to gain understanding and to learn to love his creator. And he observes carefully the variety of the creatures and their ways of mating, the skills of the nesting birds, the woodland flowers and their colors. His intimate knowledge of these things authenticates his wonder at them and his sense of the miraculousness of their existence. His wonder involves a tenderness unlike any other that I know: Of the flowers, the stones, and the stars only Kynde "himself" knows the causes; He is the magpie's patron and tells her, "putteth it in hir ere," to build her nest where the thorns are thickest.[48]

Langland and Chaucer both died in 1400. After them, I have in mind poems by Milton and Pope, in which they seem to have remembered Alan's Nature or Chaucer's or Spenser's and called her, so to speak, by name.

John Milton's *Comus* is a masque, an elegant play in verse, presented at Ludlow Castle in 1634 when the poet was twenty-five years old. It tells the story of a temptation, remembering the story of Satan's temptation of Christ (Matthew 4:1–11), and anticipating *Paradise Regained*, first published in 1671. As Spenser in the Mutability cantos had asked on what terms we are to live with the perpetual changing of this world, a question that had become urgent for him in the latter part of his life, so Milton in *Comus* was asking a question no doubt urgent in his youth but approximately parallel to Spenser's: On what terms are we to live with the material abundance of this world? Human nature, by any honest measure, is limited strictly and narrowly — we don't live very long, and we don't know very much — whereas the nature of the world at large by comparison seems a limitless plenitude. The two poets, then, were asking how to make human sense, a *little* sense, of an immensity.

In *Comus* a young maiden, identified simply as "The Lady," becomes lost in the woods. Alone and vulnerable, she meets Comus, perhaps the Tempter himself, disguised as a shepherd, who offers to guide her to safety. Instead, he takes her to "a stately palace, set out with all manner of deliciousness: soft music, tables spread with all dainties."[49] He then proves himself the masterful and eloquent seducer he really is. He makes the conventional argument of *carpe diem*, "seize the day," which Jonson, Waller, Herrick, and Marvell also made in famous poems of elegant wit, giving to their dire and perfect logic a characteristic lightness of heart. The poet, as would-be lover, reminds his lady, as Marvell would put it, that "The grave's a fine and private place, / But none, I think, do there embrace."

This is exactly Comus's argument, but he makes it with a philosophic impudence and gravity that greatly enlarges its bearing. Milton's poem is sometimes described as a defense of "the sage / And serious doctrine of Virginity."[50] It is that, but also far more than that. The poem's great question, as Comus himself raises it, is about the proper use and care of natural gifts:

> Wherefore did Nature pour her bounties forth
> With such a full and unwithdrawing hand,
> Covering the earth with odors, fruits, and flocks,
> Thronging the seas with spawn innumerable,
> But all to please and sate the curious taste?
> . . . .
>   If all the world
> Should in a pet of temperance feed on pulse,

> Drink the clear stream, and nothing wear but frieze,
> The All-giver would be unthanked, would be unpraised,
> Not half his riches known, and yet despised . . .[51]

He eventually takes up the conventional *carpe diem* theme of the transience of mortal beauty and roses that wither, but he is arguing, as the Lady quickly understands, not for using the world but for using it up. His ideology goes beyond mere personal gluttony and lust to a modern avarice and utilitarianism: the assumption, laid bare in our own time, that all of the natural world that we humans do not consume either is worthless or is wasted.

The lady, threatened by Comus's passionate intensity and his power of enchantment, is protected only by her inner light — even Comus can see that "something holy lodges in that breast[52] — and her hope of rescue, which eventually comes, but she easily overmatches Comus as a debater, arguing from a better premise and with sufficient courage. Nature, she says,

> Means her provision only to the good,
> That live according to her sober laws
> And holy dictate of spare Temperance.
> If every just man that now pines with want
> Had but a moderate and beseeming share
> Of that which lewdly-pampered luxury
> Now heaps upon some few with vast excess,
> Nature's full blessings would be well dispensed
> In unsuperfluous even proportion . . .[53]

Comus and the Lady are too allegorical in character to allow for much in the way of drama, but I don't think Milton can be accused of rigging their debate. He seems to have taken care to make Comus's argument as attractive as a vital man of twenty-five would have known it to be. The lady's argument, attractive in a way perfectly opposite, more soundly appreciative of Nature's abundance, and approving temperance as the only safeguard of abundance, is Christian and democratic. (The "Christian conservatives" of our day would call it socialism.) Her argument serves my own by what I take to be its completion of the poets' long-evolving characterization of Nature. The Lady enlarges the import of Nature's demand upon humanity by making it, at last, explicitly economic. It remained for Milton to perceive clearly that Nature requires of us a *practical* reverence. Temperance in the use of natural gifts is certainly a religious obligation, but it is also an economic virtue. *Comus* requires us to think of the right use of gifts. To be in one's right mind is to know the right use of gifts. The Lady reacts so fiercely to Comus's proposition, not just because it assaults her personal virtue, but because it disdains and destroys the idea of economy. The word "economy," taken literally, as I am taking it, does not designate a financial system, but rather the management and care of the given means of life.

. . .

Alexander Pope was a poet in many ways unlike John Milton, and yet from the Lady's rebuke to Comus it is only a step to certain poems and passages of Pope. In spite of his physical debilities, Pope had more fun than Milton, but he certainly would have recognized his kinship to the Lady in *Comus*. As the Lady puts it, the human obligation to Nature is defined by obedience "to her sober laws" and the "holy dictate" of temperance. To Pope, that obligation is defined by "Sense" or "Good Sense," which in his use of those terms is pretty much the same. As he understood her, Nature requires of us certain proprieties, not only of manners but also of work. To him, everything depended on a proper sense of scale. We must act and work with the awareness always of the magnitude of Nature's work and of our own comparative smallness as individuals and as a species. And so Pope was another enemy of prodigality, of ostentation and the utter silliness of every kind of extravagance or waste.

In the "Epistle to Burlington," his satire is against the owners of country estates who surround themselves with houses and gardens magnificent to the point of ugliness and discomfort, far exceeding in dimensions and cost any use or pleasure: "huge heaps of littleness" built to display the wealth of the owner, who by comparison is "A puny insect, shiv'ring at a breeze."[54] This is contrary to "Good Sense, which only is the gift of Heaven"[55] and is worth as much as all the sciences. Against the Prodigals who waste their wealth on expensive, fashionable things they don't even like, and especially against their grotesque extravagances in what we now call "landscaping," Pope lays down two rules —"In all, let Nature never be forgot" and "Consult the Genius of the Place in all"[56] — that my friend Wes Jackson and I have quoted back and forth for years in confirmation of our efforts for good husbandry of the land.

I need to confess, however, that I have often wondered how seriously I ought to take, not Pope's rules, which I think are sound, but Pope himself as a critic of land use. In the "Epistle to Burlington," after all, he is talking about the country houses and pleasure gardens of wealthy gentlemen, not working farms and forests. He goes so far as to say that even the worst examples, which he curses for "lavish cost, and little skill,"[57] are pardonable at least for giving employment to the poor — too much as polluting industries now are justified by "job creation."

I forgive him for that because of his prophecy, clearly hopeful and immediately following, that these show places of extravagant littleness in "another age" will be wheat fields.[58] Moreover, his understanding of the relation of art and nature is authentically complex and practical, appropriate to land use of any kind. Good sense leads to a proper mindfulness of Nature, which leads to collaboration between Nature and the gardener. The gardener's intention or design is completed by Nature's gathering of the parts into wholeness. By her gift, moreover, the land is made useful:

> 'Tis Use alone that sanctifies expense,
> And Splendor borrows all her rays from Sense.[59]

The lawns of the estate should not be ashamed to be grazed by livestock, or the beautiful forests to yield timber. Though with less passion and not so explicitly, Pope thus consents to Milton's argument in *Comus*, that the human economy should be appropriate to the human dependence on Nature.

.   .   .

Pope is the last of the English poets to be mindful of Nature as mother, maker, teacher, giver of patterns and standards, and judge — so far as I know. I have repeatedly acknowledged the limits of my knowledge, first as a duty, but also with the hope that my deficiencies will be supplied by better scholars. What I am sure of is that we have lost the old apprehension of Nature as a being accessible to imagination, linking Heaven and Earth, making and informing the incarnate creation, and requiring of humanity an obedience at once worshipful, ethical, and economic. Her stern instruction, never disproved, that we humans have a rightful but responsible place in the order of things, has disappeared, and has been absent a long time from our working consciousness and our formal schooling.

Nature, as she appeared to Chaucer, Spenser, Milton, and Pope, does not appear in the "nature poetry" of the Romantic poets, and she is absent from the history of their influence upon both poetry and the conservation movement. By the time we come to Wordsworth, who often wrote about the natural world and often was on foot in it, there is already a powerful sense of being alienated from it, with a concomitant longing to escape into it from "the din / Of towns and cities," "the heavy and the weary weight / Of all this unintelligible world," "the fretful stir / Unprofitable, and the fever of the world."[60]

I am quoting now from the poem familiarly called "Tintern Abbey," which displays pretty fully our modern love for nature, our often-lamented distance from it, and the vacationer's sensibility and economy that bring us occasionally "close" to it again, allowing us to feel more or less a religious sense of beauty and peace.

In "Tintern Abbey," addressed to his sister, Dorothy, who accompanied him, the poet has returned after a five-year absence to the Wye valley, "a wild secluded scene" of "beautiful forms," where the weight of the busy world is lightened and

> with an eye made quiet by the power
> Of harmony, and the deep power of joy,
> We see into the life of things.[61]

In the quiet and beauty of that "wild" place he feels or perhaps recalls

> A presence that disturbs me with the joy
> Of elevated thoughts; a sense sublime
> Of something far more deeply interfused,
> Whose dwelling is the light of setting suns . . .[62]

There can be no doubt of the strength of his emotion here, or of the loftiness of his language. Perhaps the presence he feels is that of Nature as the older poets imagined her, but these lines, however intense, are vague by comparison, and his thought is entirely dissipated by his resort to "something." His claim, soon following, that he recognizes

> In nature and the language of the sense
> The anchor of my purest thoughts, the nurse,
> The guide, the guardian of my heart, and soul
> Of all my moral being[63]

is devoid of any particular thought or any implication of a practical responsibility. His version of "nature" thus lacks altogether the intelligence and moral energy of Nature as she appeared to the older poets. Of Wordsworth she seems to have required nothing at all in particular, except perhaps his admiration.

In line 122 the poet personifies Nature by capitalizing her name, but he then also sentimentalizes her:

> Nature never did betray
> The heart that loved her; 'tis her privilege,
> Through all the years of this our life, to lead
> From joy to joy . . .[64]

and thus she becomes the poet's guardian against human evils and "The dreary intercourse of daily life . . ."[65] To perceive in Nature this favoritism is clearly more self-indulgent and less true than Spenser's characterization of her as the "equall mother" of all creatures, which conforms exactly to Jesus's reminder that God "maketh his sun to rise on the evil and on the good, and sendeth rain on the just and on the unjust."[66] Since Nature is so exceptionally kind to Wordsworth and his sister, it is in a manner logical that he declares himself a "worshipper of Nature."[67] Here he departs maybe as far as possible from the Nature of his predecessors, to whom she was God's vicar and thus forever subordinate to Him. The older poets were, as C. S. Lewis said of Spenser, Christians, not pantheists.

In comparison to the imaginative force and complexity of the earlier poets, this poem looks simple-minded and slack. Nature is understood merely as the purveyor of a sort of consolation or what we now call "mental health." Nobody could take from this version of Nature any sense of our economic dependence upon her, much less of her dependence upon our virtue. The wonder is that this poem contains in lines 11–17 a fine and moving description of an economic landscape —"pastoral farms / Green to the very door," "plots of cottage ground," orchards, and hedge rows — but he makes no approach to the economic life of that place or to its farmers, who certainly could have enlightened him about Nature's special preferences and favors. In this poem, the farms rate only as scenery, as they do for nature lovers of our own time.

A further wonder is that two years later Wordsworth wrote "Michael," a poem that penetrates the scenery. In that poem, the poet imagines in plenitude of detail the lives of a "pastoral" family of the Lake District: Michael, an elderly shepherd, Isabel, his wife, younger by twenty years, and their late-born only son, Luke. They live in difficult country, in weather that can be harsh. Like the many generations of their forebears, they live by endless work, from daylight to dusk and on into the night, the aging parents

> neither gay perhaps,
> Nor cheerful, yet with objects and with hopes,
> Living a life of eager industry.[68]

There is something of the quality of legend in the telling, for their life was old in the poet's memory, and old beyond memory. But I think there is little if any idealization, no "romanticizing." Above all, Wordsworth passed unregarding the temptation to present these people as "clowns" or, as we would say, "hicks." Michael's mind "was keen, intense, and frugal." As a shepherd, he is "prompt / And watchful." He knows "the meaning of all winds."[69]

The poem tells of Luke's upbringing, during which he learned his people's world and their work by accompanying his father almost from infancy, by being "Something between a hindrance and a help" at the age of five in helping his father to manage their sheep flock, and by becoming his father's "companion" in the work by the age of ten.[70]

Theirs is a "world" in itself almost complete and everlasting. But when Luke is eighteen trouble comes from the outside, as trouble is apt to come from the outside in, for instance, the novels of Thomas Hardy. Michael has mortgaged his land "in surety for his brother's son,"[71] to whom misfortune has come, and Michael is called upon to pay the debt, which amounts in value to about half his property. To preserve the land undivided as Luke's inheritance, his old parents decide to send him away, to work for another kinsman, "A prosperous man, / Thriving in trade."[72] Working for this man, Luke would earn enough to lift the debt from the land. As Michael says to Isabel,

> He quickly will repair this loss, and then
> He may return to us. If here he stay,
> What can be done? Where everyone is poor,
> What can be gained?[73]

For a time, Luke does well, the kinsman is pleased with him, he writes "loving letters" home.[74] And then doom falls with terrible swiftness upon the family and their long history:

> Luke began
> To slacken in his duty; and, at length,
> He in the dissolute city gave himself
> To evil courses: ignominy and shame
> Fell on him, so that he was driven at last
> To seek a hiding-place beyond the seas.[75]

Thus an ancient story receives almost abruptly its modern version: The Prodigal, the far-wandering son, does not now finally make his way home to continue the family lineage in its home place. Now he is gone forever. The forsaken parents live on alone, and die, and the land, at such great cost held to, is sold "into a stranger's hand."[76]

In "Tintern Abbey," without of course intending to do so, Wordsworth laid out pretty fully the model of industrial-age conservation, which reduces too readily to the effort to preserve "wilderness" and "the wild," in certain favored places, as if to compensate or forget the ongoing industrial devastation of the other landscapes. This version of conservation, industrial and romantic, orthodox and dominant for at least a century, simplifies and sentimentalizes nature as friendly, wild, virgin, spectacular or scenic, picturesque or photogenic, distant or remote from work or workplaces, ever-pleasing, consoling, restorative of a kind of norm of human sanity. Conservationists of this order have thus established and ratified a division, even a hostility between nature and our economic life that is both utterly false and limitlessly destructive of the world that they are intent upon "saving." Such conservationists are no threat at all to the economy of industry, science, and technology, of recreational equipment and vacations, which threatens everything those conservationists think they are defending, including "wilderness" and "the wild." Meanwhile the absolute dependence, even of our present so-called economy, even of our lives, upon the natural world is ignored. In my many years of advocacy for better care of farms and working forests, the silence of conservationists and their organizations has been conspicuous. They oppose sensational abuses such as global warming or fracking or (sometimes) surface mining, but they don't oppose bad farming. Most of them would not recognize bad farming if they saw it, and they see plenty of it even from the highways as they drive toward the virgin forests and the snowcapped mountains. It seems never to have occurred to them that soil erosion and stream pollution in agricultural lands threaten all of this natural world, even "the wild," and that such abuses are caused by an economy that ruins farmers and farms by policy.

"Tintern Abbey" is an archetypal poem for it gives us the taste, tone, and "spiritual" justification of the escapist nature-love of the many romantic nature poems that descended from it, and of the still-prevailing mentality of conservation. "Michael" also is an archetypal poem, but in a sense nearly opposite. Wordsworth understood it as no more than a family tragedy. Two centuries later, we must see it as uncannily predictive of millions of versions of its story all over the world: the great and consequential tragedy, little acknowledged or understood, of the broken succession of farm families, farm communities, and the cultures of husbandry. Generation after generation the children of farm couples have moved away, leaving the land's human memory, often of great ecological and economic worth, to die with their parents. Whether they have gone away to fail or succeed by the measures of their time, they still have gone away, and their absence is a permanent and enormous loss. And so "Michael" is great both because of its achievement and stature as a work of art and because of its rarity and significance as a cultural landmark. It stands high among the poems that have meant most to me. I first read it more than sixty years ago.

The second tragedy of "Michael" has to do with the history of the poem itself. Unlike "Tintern Abbey," it has had, so far as I am aware, no influence on our thinking about the natural world and our use of it, and little or no influence on the subsequent history of poetry. It stands almost alone. The only poem I know that I think worthy of its company is "Marshall Washer," by my friend Hayden Carruth. Marshall Washer was for many years Hayden's neighbor, a dairy farmer near Johnson, Vermont. Like Michael, Marshall lived a life of hard work on a small farm in a demanding place and climate. As, like Michael, the master and artist of his circumstances, Marshall earned Hayden's love and respect, and from his companionship and example Hayden learned many things that he valued. Hayden, moreover, saw Marshall in perspective of the hard history of such farmers before and after the time of Wordsworth. In the poem, Marshall has lived and worked and aged into a loneliness known to millions of his kind and time. His wife has died, and his sons have

> departed, caring little for the farm because
> he had educated them — he who left school
> in 1931 to work by his father's side
> on an impoverished farm in an impoverished time.[77]

Beyond Marshall's life, the life of the farm had become unknowable and unimaginable, and all such farms were coming under the influence of "development." Land prices and taxes were increasing. It was becoming less possible for a small farmer to own a small farm. And Hayden imagined Marshall's sorrow:

> farming is an obsolete vocation —
> while half the world goes hungry. Marshall walks

his fields and woods, knowing every useful thing
about them, and knowing his knowledge useless.[78]

This describes the breaking of what Hayden called "the link of the
manure"—"manure" in the senses both of fertilizing and caring for,
hand-working, the land — which cannot be ignorantly maintained.
The "link of the manure" is the fundamental economic link between
humans and the natural world. No matter the plain necessity of this
link, it is breaking, or is broken, everywhere.

Ignorance certainly will break it. But so also will forces imposed
upon it by what we falsely and too readily think of as the "larger"
economy. There obviously can be no economy larger than its own
natural sources and supports. Less obvious, farming being "an obsolete
vocation" as far as most of us are concerned, is the impossibility that
any economy can be larger or more important or more valuable than
the economies of land use that connect us practically to the natural
sources. Nevertheless, we have this small contrivance we call "the econ-
omy," utterly detached from our households and our need for food,
clothing, and shelter, in which people "put their money to work for
them" and sit down to await the increase, in which money interbreed-
ing with money enlarges itself to monstrosity, glutting on the world's
goods. This small economy, centralized and concentrated in the larger
cities, imposes in its great equation of ignorance and power a deter-
mining and limitlessly destructive influence upon the economies of
land use, of farming and forestry, which are large, dispersed, and weak.

Those of us who would like to understand this could do worse than
consult with poets, or with the too few of them who have taken an
interest and paid attention. Those two widely separated and lonely
poems, "Michael" and "Marshall Washer," are tragedies of the modern
world. The stories they tell become tragic because the interest of the

land, the human investment of interest and affection in the land, becomes subordinated to the interest of a "larger" economy that removes the human interest native to a place and replaces it with its own interest in itself.

. . .

After the story of the westward migration, the dominant American story so far is that of the young people who have departed from their rural birthplaces, "humble" or "small" or "backward" or "poor," to find success or failure in the big city. The story of the loneliness of the elders left behind, though surely as common, is rarely told. The implication of its rarity is that it does not matter, but is only a small sorrow incidental to the quest for a greater happiness. But sometimes a backward look will occur, bringing a recognition of loss and suffering that matter more than expected. The example I have in mind is a Carter Family song, "The Homestead on the Farm":

> I wonder how the old folks are at home,
> I wonder if they miss me when I'm gone,
> I wonder if they pray for the boy who went away
> And left his dear old parents all alone.[79]

The song, which I like, carries the story only as far as nostalgia: The departed boy looks back with fondness for his old home, which his memory no doubt has improved, and with some regret, but he clearly has no plans to return. Maybe we can do no better than this, having as yet no common standards or a common language to deal with social disintegration, much less with diminishments of culture and the loss of local memory, all of which will enter into an accounting indivisibly cultural, ecological, and economic.

. . .

I don't know if Ezra Pound ever actually knew such people as Michael or Marshall Washer. But his poems on usury, "sin against nature," cast on the stories of these men what has been for me an indispensable light. Maybe nobody ever gave more passionate attention than Pound to the ability of a monetary system by means of usury to drive the cost of land and its products beyond any human measure of their worth, and thus to prey upon and degrade the work and the health that sustain us. And nobody has ever instructed us about this with more economy or grace or beauty:

> With usury has no man a good house
> made of stone, no paradise on his church wall
> With usury the stonecutter is kept from his stone
> the weaver is kept from his loom by usura
> Wool does not come into market
> the peasant does not eat his own grain
> The girl's needle goes blunt in her hand
> The looms are hushed one after another
> . . . .
> Usury kills the child in the womb
> And breaks short the young man's courting
> Usury brings age into youth; it lies between the bride
> and the bridegroom
> Usury is against Nature's increase.[80]

Pound had the misfortune, self-induced, of becoming more notorious for his prejudices and political mistakes than famous for sanity. But he did have in him a broad streak of good sense. He could see all the way to the ground, not invariably a talent among poets, and he had moments of incisive agrarianism. He wrote in these lines a clarifying history of modern land husbandry:

Dress 'em in folderols
    and feed 'em with dainties,
In the end they will sell out the homestead.[81]

He praised with perfect soundness "Chao-Kong the surveyor" who "Gave each man land for his labour"[82] — wages being always vulnerable, whereas the value of land, like the value of a life, is unreckonable and absolute. And he wrote these lines,

Pull down thy vanity, I say pull down.
Learn of the green world what can be thy place
In scaled invention or true artistry...[83]

in which he stood before Nature much in the posture of Alan of Lille eight hundred years before.

.   .   .

Whoever would think at the same time of the home ecosystem on the one hand, and on the other of the home community (ecosystem plus humans), is all but forced to think of the local economy — and its tributary local economies elsewhere. Very few poets — very few people — have thought of both at once, because, I suppose, of the intensity of the stretch. It is something like standing with one foot on shore and the other in a loosely floating small boat. It requires a big heart and a strong crotch.

Of the poets I know of my own time, Gary Snyder is the one whose thought and work (in poetry and prose) have most insistently inclined toward the daily and practical issues of our economic life, which is to say our life: the possibility of bringing our getting and spending into concordance with terrestrial reality. This has been, for Gary, a lifelong effort, involving the events and materials of his life, much travel, much reading, much study and thought of his home geography. At a loss as to how to represent this effort in its complexity, I will say only that I think it has begun and renewed itself again and again in realizations of the profound, indissoluble link, the virtual identity, between the world's life and the lives of creatures. How is it with us who live our ever-changing lives as parts or members of the ever-changing world? Or to use language Gary has borrowed from Dogen: How is it with us who are walking on mountains that are walking? This question is not comfortable, and we sometimes would like to ignore or wish against it. But it means at least that the world is always with us, new and fresh:

> Clear running stream
>   clear running stream
>
> Your water is light
>   to my mouth
> And a light to my dry body
>
>   your flowing
> Music,
>   in my ears. free,
>
> Flowing free!
> With you
>   in me.[84]

It is not hard to imagine thoughts of economy and of "the economy" starting from the tenderness, intimacy, and inherent delight of this kindness, this kinship. But the poem also is a thanksgiving, the proper conclusion to such thoughts.

And I ask myself, Can it be that, by way of Buddhism and American

Indian anthropology, Gary Snyder is another who has come face to face with the great goddess, great dame Nature, and he makes her this cordial greeting? Maybe.

.   .   .

It must be clear enough by now that I am a reader who reads for instruction. I have always read, even literature, even poetry, for instruction. I am a poet, and so I have read other poets as a poet, to learn about poetry, and, just as important, to learn from poetry. I am also in a small way a farmer devoted to farming, as my father and his father made me, and I have read poetry, and everything else, also as a farmer. As a farmer I have lived daily with the inherent hardships and pleasures, but also with an ever-fascinating and utterly intimidating question: What should I be doing to care properly for this (as it happens) very difficult and demanding place? And a further one: How can I make myself a man capable of seeing what is the right thing to do, and of doing it?

Such questions now are typically addressed to experts, and are answered by a letter or a pamphlet replete with statistics, graphs, diagrams, and instructions, all presumed to be applicable to all persons and to any and every place within a designated region or zone. This may in fact prove helpful, but it is not enough. It is not enough because it includes no knowledge of the particular and unique place where the expertise is to be applied. Moreover, expertise which is credentialed and much dependent on the demeanor and language of authority is typically unable to acknowledge either its inner ignorance or the immense mystery that surrounds equally the asker and the answerer. And so askers are in effect left alone with the expert answer on their singular small places within the mostly uninformative universe.

Supplements and alternatives are available. One can talk with one's neighbors and elders, who never are oracles but are usually worth listening to. One can consult with other experts. I have always liked to consult older or earlier experts, whose knowledge may be seasoned with affection and humility. Or one can read, following one's nose as good hounds and readers do, always on watch for what people in other times and places have known or learned, what penalties they paid for ignorance, what satisfactions they gained by knowledge. These benefits can come from books of every kind.

Such broad and even random conversation is necessary because the present industrial world is not an isolated empire fortified against history or incomparable by its improvements with other times and ways. As I have conversed and read for the last fifty years, I have been reminding myself that many new ways of doing work have been adopted not because they were better for land and people, but simply because the old ways were technologically outmoded. Industrial agriculture, as probably the paramount example, is better than pre-industrial agriculture by the standard mainly of corporate profitability, excluding by a sort of conventional or fashionable blindness the paramount standard of mental, bodily, and ecological health. One can learn this by the study of rural landscapes, but conversation and reading also are necessary. To think responsibly about land use, the whole known spectrum of means and ways must be available to one's thoughts. If, for example, one cannot compare a tractor (and its attendant economy and ecological effects) with a team of horses (and its attendant economy and ecological effects), then one has the use of less than half of one's mind.

Do I, then, think that farmers, or persons of other vocations, can find actual help in reading Chaucer or Milton or Spenser or Pope? Yes, that is what I think. To know Chaucer's plowman is not to know something merely of historical interest. It is to know, to recognize immediately, something that one needs to know. It would be too much to say that *all* farmers, foresters, economists, ecologists, and conservationists should know what Chaucer, Spenser, Milton, and Pope wrote about Nature, but it is a pity and a danger that none or only a few of them do.

· · ·

Having argued that it is possible to learn valuable, even useful and necessary things from poetry, I now have to answer two further questions. First: Is it necessary for a poem to be instructive in order to be good? I hope not, and I don't think so. There is nothing very instructive, for example, in hearing that "the cow jumped over the moon," but who is not delighted by that poem's exuberant indifference to the possibility of making sense? It is a masterpiece. Even so, I am happy to know that some poems delight *and* instruct, which is a richer possibility.

Second: How does an instructive poem instruct? The answer seems obvious — by containing something worth knowing — but there is one condition: It must teach without intending to do so. In support of this I offer a sentence by Jacques Maritain, who said of the cathedral builders: "Their achievement revealed God's truth, but without *doing it on purpose*, and because it was not done on purpose."[85] The point, I believe, is that what the cathedral builders were doing on purpose was building a cathedral. Any other purpose would have distracted them from the thing they were making and spoiled their work. Teaching as a purpose, as such, is difficult to prescribe or talk about because the thing it is proposing to make is usually something so vague as "understanding." My own best teachers, as I remember, sometimes undertook deliberately to teach me something: "You handed me that board wrong, and made my work harder. Now I'm going to hand it back to you *right*. Now you hand it back to me *right*." But this was rare. When I was most learning from them, I think, they were attempting something besides teaching, if only to make a sentence that made sense. They taught me best by example, unaware that they were teaching or that I was learning. Just so, an honest poet who is making a poem is doing neither more nor less than making a poem, undistracted by the thought even that it will be read. Poets, or some poets, bear witness as faithfully as possible to what they have experienced or observed, suffered or enjoyed, and this inevitably is instructive to anybody able to be instructed. But the instruction is secondary. It must be embodied in the work.

.   .   .

One remarkable thing I have noticed in my reading is that agrarianism, readily identifiable by certain themes (the importance of the small holding, the relationship to Nature, etc.), appears throughout the written record from as far back as Homer and the Bible. A second remarkable thing is that these appearances are intermittent, sometime widely separated. When this vital strand of human thought and concern has disappeared from writing — as it does, in poetry, from Wordsworth's "Michael" to Hayden Carruth's "Marshall Washer"— it has continued in the conversation of farmers. I was (I am still) Hayden Carruth's friend. I knew him from much conversation and many letters. In Hayden's company I met and talked at some length with Marshall Washer. Though Hayden was far better read than I am, I am confident that the agrarianism of Hayden's poem did not come from his reading. It came straight from Marshall himself, who had it from his father who had it from a lineage of living voices going back and back, more or less parallel to, but rarely, maybe never, intersecting with the lineage of writings. I know this also from my own long participation in such conversation. The appearances of agrarian thought in the written record are like stepping stones, separate and irregularly spaced, but resting on a firm and (so far) a continuous bottom.

Who were, and to a much-reduced extent still are, the people who have passed this tradition by living word from generation to generation for so long? The answer, obviously, is the country people who have done the work of field and forest, generation after generation. They are the people once known as peasants, serfs, or churls, and now, still doing the same work, as farmers or country people, when "farmer" and "country" are still as readily used as terms of abuse as "peasant" and "churl" ever were. My friend Gene Logsdon says that when he was a schoolboy in Wyandot County, Ohio, "Dumb farmer was one word."

Here I need to remember two sentences from G. G. Coulton's *Medieval Panorama*. The first is this: "Four-fifths, at least, of the medieval population had grown their own food in their own fields; had spun and woven wool from their own sheep or linen from their own toft; and very often it was they themselves who made it into clothes."[86] I should add that they also kept themselves housed, and they fed and sheltered their animals. Anybody who has done any part of such work knows that it involves knowledge of the highest order and value, for the human species has survived by it, and it is neither simple nor easy to learn.

But how were these people with their elaborate and indispensable knowledge valued in the Middle Ages? Here is the second sentence from *Medieval Panorama*: "Froissart shows us plainly enough how, after the bloody capture of a town or castle, the gentles [knights and nobles] were spared, but the common soldiers [churls] were massacred without protest from their more exalted comrades in arms."[87] They were thought to be, in a word, dispensable.

I don't believe that this thought has changed very substantially from then until now. We, whose humane instincts have so famously evolved and improved, are firmly opposed to outmoded forms of massacre, but we still regard farmers as dispensable, and by various economic constraints and social fashions we have dispensed with many millions of them over the last sixty or so years. If the twenty-first-century American farmer is farming several thousand acres and employing a million dollars' worth of equipment, he still is a member of a disparaged, and therefore a vanishing, population. He does not control any part of his economy. He has no more influence over the markets on which he buys and sells than he has over the weather. No prominent politician, economist, or intellectual is thoughtful either of him or of the condition of the land he works, or of the health of the ecosystem that includes his land. In the entire food industry he will be dependably the most at risk, the least valued, and the lowest paid, except, of course, for the migrant laborers he may at times be constrained to hire. If he miscalculates or has a bad year and is ruined, that will register among the professional onlookers as a minor instance of "creative destruction."

In the course of this progress of industrialization and depopulation, farming itself has become so radically simplified as to be unworth the name. Most damaging has been the division between the field crop industry and the meat-animal industry. To remove the farm animals from farming is to remove more than half of the need for knowledge, skill, and intelligence, and nearly all of the need for sympathy. To crowd the animals into the tightest possible confinement to live and function exclusively as meat-makers is to do away with sympathy as a precondition, to reduce mindfulness to routine, and to replace all the free helps of Nature and natural health with purchased machinery and medicines.

But when plants and animals, croplands and pastures, are gathered into the care of a single farmer, this calls for a mind versatile and accomplished, competent to deal with the fairly stable natures of the kinds of plants and animals, as well as the variable and sometimes surprising circumstances of mortality, the weather, and the economy. Among the good farmers I have known, I have found also a formal intelligence by which they ordered the spatial arrangement of fences, fields, and buildings to be most conserving of the land and most usable, and by which they formed also the temporal structures of their crop rotations and the days, seasons, and years of their work.

Good farmers, whose minds are comparable to the minds of artists of the "fine arts," have been instructed so often for so long that they are "dumbfarmers" that they only half believe how smart and capable they actually are. I have heard too many of them describe themselves as "just a farmer." It is, at any rate, impossible for highly credentialed professionals and academics to appraise justly the intelligence of a good farmer. They are too ignorant for that. You might as well send a bird dog to judge the competence of a neurologist.

About such things there are no "objective" measures. I can offer only my testimony. In my by-now long life, I have known well and observed closely the work of a good many farmers whom I have respected. I have thought carefully about them for a long time, and some of them I have written about. In general: I have found them alert, observant, interested, interesting, thoughtful of their experience, conversant with the experience of others. By midlife or sooner they have come to know many things so completely as to be unconscious of knowing them. They have had, in general, the humorous intelligence that recognizes natural limits and their own limits. They have had also a commonplace sense of tragedy that permitted them to accept their helplessness in the face of loss and suffering — as Marshall Washer faced his burning barn with thirteen heifers trapped inside, and kept on, still working, by the testimony of his friend Hayden Carruth, within weeks of his death at eighty-eight. That is not indicative either of "dullness" or "stoicism," nor does it mean that farmers in general are better or more virtuous than other persons. It means simply that farmers live and work in circumstances unremittingly practical and for this certain strengths of mind are necessary.

In general, the good farmers I have known have had no taste for self-display, did not parade their knowledge, and would say little where their knowledge might not be respected. But if you had a mind and ear for their conversation, and some ground of friendship or common knowledge, you were likely to hear sound sense that came from their experience of the natural world, and of farming and its local history. As late as my own generation, because the young then were still working with and listening to their elders, the talk of farmers was still carrying the traditional themes and attitudes. Many of the things I heard from them I have kept always in my mind, their words and their voices.

.   .   .

Probably in the summer of 1965, after my family and I had moved here to the "twelve acres more or less" where we still live, I was not equipped for some mowing that needed to be done. I hired a neighbor of my parents' generation, a man I had known from my childhood, liked, and respected. When he had finished the work, he turned off the tractor engine and we talked a while, he much in the spirit of welcoming me to my new place. He had been renewing his own acquaintance with the place as he worked. We spoke of the ways it had been used (not always kindly), and of the uses I might make of it.

When he was ready to go, he started the tractor and, to end the conversation, said cheerfully, "Well, try a little of everything, you'll hit on something."

He knew, and he knew I knew, how little of "everything" the old place was actually capable of producing on its steep slopes and its one pretty good "garden spot" by the river. But he had said a good thing, and we both knew that. He had stated one of Nature's laws: the Law of Diversity, vital both to ecological and to economic health. One of my father's father's rules was "Sell something every week," a different version of the Law of Diversity.

Another of my older friends, a fine farmer whose friendship I inherited from my father, once told me a crucial part of the story of his beginning on his own farm. This, I think, would have been in 1940 or a little earlier. He and his wife had gone into debt to buy their place, and they had no money. My friend went early in the year to a grocery store in town and asked the owner if he would "carry" him until he sold his crop. The owner knew him, trusted him, and agreed. When my friend sold his crop at the year's end and went to settle up at the store, his bill came to eleven dollars and some cents. He and his wife had been thrifty and careful, living so far as possible from their place, thus obeying another of Nature's laws, the Law of Frugality: Don't be prodigal.

A man of about the same age, a dear friend who was conscientiously my teacher for thirty years, once told me with an emphasis amounting to passion: "If you've got grass and room to keep a milk cow [for family use] and you don't do it, you've *lost* one milk cow." The absent cow he saw, not as a neutral matter of mere preference, but as a negative economic force, a subtraction from thrift and thriving. This was in respect for the Law of Diversity and the Law of Frugality.

A steadying influence on my mind for most of my life has been the metaphor by which my father referred to a patch of abused land that had been healed and grassed as "haired over." He thus perceived a wound to the earth as a wound to a living creature, perhaps a collar gall on the shoulder of a workhorse. We could say that this phrase observes another of Nature's laws — Keep the ground covered — but much else of value is concentrated in it. By it my father wakened my mind to the thought of the system of kinships by which the world survives, and to the thought of the whole significance of the smallest healing. I don't know whether or not this language originated with my father, but I knew *his* father and so I know that it was not the thought of one mind. Such a thought is as far as possible unlike the thought of the earth as an inert material mass to be shoved about, poisoned, and blasted at human discretion.

None of those sayings comes from a note I made at the time or from any record I kept, but only from memory, and to me this signifies their importance and value. I have remembered them and many others, I believe, because I recognized them not quite consciously as parts of a whole, a kind of mind which, like my mentors, I inherited, which probably is as old as farming and necessary to it. This mind, which I think has never been fully conscious or coherent in any one person, never perfect, always in some manner failing, almost never having the incentive of public appreciation or adequate economic support, has nonetheless cohered, coming to consciousness as needed, and expressing itself in an articulate local speech that takes its heft and inflection from the reconciliations between people and their circumstances, their work and their feelings about it. This mind, much to the credit of its inherent good sense, has survived all its adversities until now, living on, talking to itself, so to say, in the conversation of its local memberships. It still speaks, where it survives, of the importance of the well-doing of small tasks that the dominant culture has always considered degrading but which are nonetheless essential and worthy of care: "Don't think of the dollar," my friend and teacher said to me. "Think of the *job*." And it still speaks of our dependence on the particular natures of creatures and on the natural world, and, more practically, of a necessary respect and deference toward Nature. In this speech, Nature customarily is personified: the great dame herself, who knows best and will have her way. Always there is the implication that Nature helps when you work *with* her, with knowledge of her ways, their value, and their ultimate dominance, and that she does not help, but works against you when you work against her.

Recently my son brought me an issue of a conventional industrial farming magazine, containing an article, by a "semi-retired" rancher, Walt Davis, about the need to manage a cow herd so as "to be in sync with nature."[88] Though some of the vocabulary ("in sync") is new, this advice is old. I know nothing that suggests it is wrong. The point, as often, is economic: To be in sync with Nature is to make full use of her helps that are free or cheap, as opposed to the use of industrial substitutes that are expensive. By observance of Nature's laws, the land survives and even thrives in human use. By the *same* laws, farmers can hope at least to survive in the almost conventional adversity of the farm economy.

Almost typical of young farmers is the impulse to intervene in natural processes with some "latest" expertise, requiring typically some "latest" merchandise in order to increase production or fend off some perceived threat. Older farmers are more likely to be suspicious of anything that costs money, and to rely instead on the gifts of their own intelligence and the nature of creatures. Young shepherds, in their eager and self-regarding sympathy, may try to help a newborn lamb to stand and suck — may even succeed, or seem to. Older shepherds will know that such "help" is most likely a waste of time. They know when to walk away and "leave it to Nature." They are likely to know also that Nature bids them to get rid of a ewe whose lamb can survive its birth only with human help.

Going on forty years ago, because I knew his grand reputation as a breeder of Southdown sheep, I had the honor of becoming a little acquainted with Henry Besuden of Vinewood Farm in Clark County, Kentucky. Mr. Besuden was seventy-six years old then and not in good health; it had been several years since he had owned a sheep. But when I visited him, which I did at least twice, and he showed me his place and we talked at length, I found that his accomplishments as a farmer excelled in fact and in interest his accomplishments as a sheepman.[89]

In 1927, at the age of twenty-three, he inherited a farm of 632 acres, a large holding for that country, but it came to him as something less than a privilege. The land had been ruined by the constant row-cropping of renters: "Corned to death." Gullies were everywhere, some of them deep enough to hide a standing man. Between Mr. Besuden then and an inheritance of nothing was the stark need virtually to re-make his farm. To do this he had to return the land from its history of human carelessness to the care of Nature: Every gully, through which the land was flowing away, had to be transformed into a grassed swale that would check and retain the runoff. This required a lot of work and a long time, but by 1950 all of the scars at last were grassed over.

To this effort the sheep were not optional but necessary. They would thrive on the then-inferior, weedy and briary pastures, and, rightly managed, they were "land builders." He became a sheepman in order to become the farmer Nature required for his land. The constant theme of his work was "a way of farming compatible with nature" or, as Pope would have put it, with "the Genius of the place." I have not known a farmer in whose mind the traditional agrarianism was more complete or more articulate.

He wrote in one of his several articles entitled "Sheep Sense": "It is good to have Nature working for you. She works for a minimum wage." Soil conservation, he wrote, "also involves the heart of the man managing the land. If he loves his soil he will save it." He wrote again, obedient to Nature's guidance, of the need "to study the possibilities of grass fattening." He wrote of the importance of "little things done on time." He told me about a farmer who would wait until he came to a spot bare of grass to scrape the manure off his shoes: "That's what I mean. You have to keep it in your mind."

. . .

In any economy that becomes exploitive of land or people or (as usual) both, it appears that some of the people working within it will recognize that its special standards of judgment are inadequate. They will see the need for a more comprehending standard by which the constrictive system can be judged, so to speak, from the outside. At present, for example, some doctors and others who work in the medical profession have the uneasy awareness that their industrial standards are failing, and their thoughts are going, as always in such instances, toward Nature's laws, which is to say, toward the health that is at once bodily, familial, communal, economic, and ecological. The outside standard invariably will turn out to be health, and perceptive people, looking beyond industrial medicine, see that health is not the painlessness of a body part, or the comfort of parts of a society. They see that the idea of a healthy individual in an unhealthy community in an unhealthy place is an absurdity that, by the standards of industry, can only become more absurd.

In agricultural science the same realization was occurring at the beginning of the twentieth century. The first prominent sign of this, so far as I know, was a book, *Farmers of Forty Centuries*, in which F. H. King, who had been professor of agricultural physics at the University of Wisconsin, recounted his travels among the small farms of China, Korea, and Japan. As a student of soil physics and soil fertility, King must be counted an expert witness, but he was also a sympathetic one. He was farm-raised, and his interest in agriculture seems to have come from a lifelong affection for farming, farmers, and the details of their work.

The impetus for his Asian journey seems to have been his recognition of the critical deficiencies of American agriculture, the chief one being the relentless exploitation of soil and soil fertility by practices that were supportable only by the importation to the farms of "cargoes of feeding stuffs and mineral fertilizers."[90] This, he knew, could not last. It was, we would say now, unsustainable, as it still is. It was possible in the United States because the United States was still a thinly populated country.

Such extravagance had never been possible in China, Korea, and

Japan, where "the people . . . are toiling in fields tilled more than three thousand years and who have scarcely more than two acres per capita, more than one-half of which is uncultivable mountain land."[91] This long-enduring agriculture was made possible by keeping the fertility cycle intact and in place. The "plant food materials" that we were wasting, "through our modern systems of sewage disposal and other faulty practices," the Asian farmers "held . . . sacred to agriculture, applying them to their fields."[92]

As a sample of the economic achievement of the peasant farms he visited, King says in his introduction that "in the Shantung province [of China] we talked with a farmer having 12 in his family and who kept one donkey, one cow, both exclusively laboring animals, and two pigs on 2.5 acres of cultivated land where he grew wheat, millet, sweet potatoes and beans."[93] The introduction ends with this summary:

Almost every foot of land is made to contribute material for food, fuel or fabric. Everything which can be made edible serves as food for man or domestic animals. Whatever cannot be eaten or worn is used for fuel. The wastes of the body, of fuel and of fabric worn beyond other use are taken back to the field . . .[94]

The chapters that follow contain finely detailed descriptions of one tiny farm after another, every one of them exemplifying what I have called Nature's Law of Frugality, or what Sir Albert Howard would later call her "law of return." Fertility, we might say, was understood as borrowed from Nature on condition of repayment in full. "Nothing," King wrote, "jars on the nerves of these people more than incurring of needless expense, extravagance in any form, or poor judgment in making purchases."[95] No debt was to be charged to the land and left unpaid, as we were doing in King's time and are doing still.

· · ·

Farmers of Forty Centuries was published in 1911. In 1929, J. Russell Smith, then professor of economic geography at Columbia University, published *Tree Crops*, another necessary book, another of my stepping stones. I don't know whether or not Smith had read King's book, but that does not matter, for Smith's book was motivated by the same trouble: our senseless waste of fertility and the prospect of land exhaustion.

What Smith saw was not only our fracture of the fertility cycle, but also another, an opposite, cycle: "Forest — field — plow — desert — that is the cycle of the hills under most plow agricultures…"[96] Smith was worried about soil erosion. He had seen a part of China that King had not visited:

> The slope below the Great Wall was cut with gullies, some of which were fifty feet deep. As far as the eye could see were gullies, gullies, gullies — a gashed and gutted countryside.[97]

And Smith knew that there were places similarly ruined in the "new" country of the United States. The mistake, everywhere, was obvious: "Man has carried to the hills the agriculture of the flat plain." The problem, more specifically, was the agriculture of annual plants. "As plants," he wrote, "the cereals are weaklings."[98] They cannot protect the ground that their cultivation exposes to the weather.

As Henry Besuden had realized on his own farm two years before the publication of Smith's book, the reaction against the damage of annual cropping could only go in the direction of perennials: Slopes that were not wooded needed to be permanently grassed. So Mr. Besuden rightly thought. J. Russell Smith took the same idea one step further: to what he called, "two-story agriculture,"[99] which would work anywhere, but which he saw as a necessity, both natural and human, for hillsides. The lower story would be grass; the upper story would consist of "tree crops" producing nuts and fruits either as forage for livestock or as food for humans.

The greater part of Smith's book is devoted to species and varieties of trees suitable for such use, and to examples (with photographic plates and explanatory captions) of two-story agriculture in various parts of the world. He was, he acknowledged, a visionary: "I see a million hills green with crop-yielding trees and a million neat farm homes snuggled in the hills."[100] But he was careful to show, by his many examples, that two-story agriculture *could* work because in some places it was working, and in some places it had been working for hundreds of years. He was promoting a proven possibility, not a theory.

Like Alan of Lille, Smith understood Nature's condemnation of prodigality, and he accepted her requirement that we should save what we have been given. The passion that informs his book comes from his realization that Nature's most precious gift was given only once. The Prodigal Son could squander his inheritance of money, repent, and be forgiven and restored to his father's favor. But Nature, "the equall mother" of all the creatures, has no bias in favor of humans. She gave us, along with all her other children, the great gift of life in a rich world, the wealth of which reduces finally to its thin layer of fertile soil. When we have squandered that, no matter how we may repent, it is simply and finally gone.

Smith was above all a practical man, and he stated one of Nature's laws in terms exquisitely practical: "*farming should fit the land.*" The italics are his. He said that this amounted to "*a new point of view,*"[101] and again his italics indicate his sense of the urgency of what he was saying. He was undoubtedly right in assuming that this point of view was new to his countrymen, or to most of them, but of course it was also very old. It was implicit in Nature's complaint to Alan of Lille, it was explicit in Virgil's first Georgic, more than a thousand years before Alan, and it certainly informed Pope's instructions to consult "the Genius of the Place." The point is that, in using land, you cannot know what you are doing unless you know well the place where you are doing it.

. . .

In the long lineage that I am discussing, the fundamental assumption appears to be that Nature is the perfect — and, for our purposes, the exemplary — proprietor and user of any of her places. In our agricultural uses of her land, we are not required to imitate her work, because, as Chaucer's physician says, she is inimitable, and in order to live we are obliged to interpose our own interest between her and her property. We are required instead to do, not *as* she does, but *what* she does to protect the land and preserve its health. For our farming in our own interest, she sets the pattern and provides the measure. We learn to farm properly only under the instruction of Nature: "What are the main principles underlying Nature's agriculture? These can most easily be seen in operation in our woods and forests."[102]

Those are the key sentences of *An Agricultural Testament*, by Sir Albert Howard, published in 1940. Howard had read *Farmers of Forty Centuries*, and his testimony begins with the worry that had sent King to Asia:

Since the Industrial Revolution the processes of growth have been speeded up to produce the food and raw materials needed by the population and the factory. Nothing effective has been done to replace the loss of fertility involved in this vast increase in crop and animal production. The consequences have been disastrous. Agriculture has become unbalanced: the land is in revolt: diseases of all kinds are on the increase: in many parts of the world Nature is removing the worn-out soil by means of erosion.[103]

From this perception of human error and failure he made the turn to Nature, that we can now recognize, across a span of many centuries, as characteristic and continuing in a lineage of some poets, some intelligent farmers and farm cultures, and some scientists. Howard's study of agriculture rests solidly upon his study of the nature of the places where farming was done. If the land in use was originally forested, as much of it was and is, then to learn to farm well, the farmer should study the forest.

Industrial agriculture, far from consulting the Genius of the Place or fitting the farming to the land or remembering at all the ecological mandate for local adaptation, has instead and from the beginning forced the land to submit to the capabilities and the limitations of the available technology. From the ruinous and ugly consequences, now visible and obvious everywhere the land can be farmed, one turns with relief to the great good sense, the mere sanity, the cheerful confidence of Howard's advice to farmers: Go to the woods and see what Nature would be doing on your land if you were not farming it, for you are asking her, not just for her "resources," but to accept you as her student and collaborator. And Howard summarizes the inevitable findings in the following remarkable paragraph:

> The main characteristic of Nature's farming can therefore be summed up in a few words. Mother earth never attempts to farm without livestock; she always raises mixed crops; great pains are taken to preserve the soil and to prevent erosion; the mixed vegetable and animal wastes are converted into humus; there is no waste; the processes of growth and the processes of decay balance one another; ample provision is made to maintain large reserves of fertility; the greatest care is taken to store the rainfall; both plants and animals are left to protect themselves against disease.[104]

Howard was familiar with the work of F. H. King and other scientific predecessors. *An Agricultural Testament*, he says, was founded upon his own "work and experience of forty years, mainly devoted to agricultural research in the West Indies, India, and Great Britain."[105] He had the humility and the good sense to learn from the peasant farmers his work was meant to serve. He came from a Shropshire farm family "of high reputation locally,"[106] and so I assume he had grown up hearing the talk of farmers. I don't know what, if anything, he had learned from the poets I have learned from, but of course I am delighted that he called Nature personally by name as Chaucer, Spenser, Milton, and Pope had done.

. . .

As Milton in *Comus* had enlarged the earlier characterizations of Nature by recognizing the economic significance of her religious and moral demands, making it explicit and practical, so the work of Sir Albert Howard completed their ecological significance. The agricultural economy, and the economies of farms, as determined by the economies and technologies of industrialism, would by logical necessity run to exhaustion. Agriculture in general, and any farm in particular, could survive only by recognizing, respecting, and incorporating the integrity of ecosystems. And this, as Howard showed by his work, could be understood practically and put into practice.

Spenser's problem of stability within change, moreover, we may think of as waiting upon Howard for its proper solution, which he gives in *The Soil and Health*, published in 1947:

It needs a more refined perception to recognize throughout this stupendous wealth of varying shapes and forms the principle of stability. Yet this principle dominates. It dominates by means of an ever-recurring cycle, a cycle which, repeating itself silently and ceaselessly, ensures the continuation of living matter. This cycle is constituted of the successive and repeated processes of birth, growth, maturity, death, and decay. An eastern religion calls this cycle the Wheel of Life and no better name could be given to it. The revolutions of this Wheel never falter and are perfect. Death supersedes life and life rises again from what is dead and decayed.[107]

As Howard of course knew, religion would construe that last sentence analogically or symbolically, but he does not diminish it or make it less miraculous by treating it as fact. The Wheel of Life, or the fertility cycle, is not an instance of stability as opposed to change, as Spenser may have hoped, but rather an instance, much more interesting and wonderful, of stability dependent upon change. The Wheel of Life is a religious principle of which Howard saw the scientific validity, or it is a principle of Nature, eventually of science, which has long been "natural" to religion. This suggests that beyond the experimental or empirical proofs of science, there may be other ways of determining the truth of a solution, a very prominent one being versatility. Is the solution valid economically as well as ecologically? Does it serve the interest both of the land and of the land's people? The Wheel of Life certainly has that double validity. But we can go on: Does it fit both the farm and the local ecosystem? Does it satisfy the needs of both biology and religion? Is it imaginatively as well as factually true? Can it reconcile utility and beauty? Is it compatible with the practice of the virtues? As a solution to the problem of change and stability, The Wheel of Life answers affirmatively every one of those questions. It is complexly, and joyously, true.

Such a solution could not have originated, and cannot be accommodated, under the rule of industrial or technological progress, which does not cycle, which recycles only under compulsion, and makes no returns. Waste is one of its definitive products, and waste is profitable so long as you are not liable for the cost or replacement of what you have wasted.

Waste of the gifts of Nature from the beginning of industrialism has subsidized our system of corporate profits and "economic growth." Howard, judging by the unforgiving standard of natural health, described this "economy" unconditionally: "The using up of fertility is a transfer of past capital and of future possibilities to enrich a dishonest present: it is banditry pure and simple."[108]

The falsehood of the industrial economy has been disguised for generations by the departmentalization and over-specialization of the essential academic and intellectual disciplines. In the absence of any common or unifying standard of judgment, the professionals of the schools have been free to measure their work by professional standards exclusively, submitting only to the "peer review" of fellow professionals. As in part a professional himself, Howard understood the ethical blindness of this system. Against it he raised the standard of the integrity of the Wheel of Life, which is comprehensive and universal, granting no exemptions.

Whether because of his "instinctive awareness of the importance of natural principle"[109] or because of respect for his own intelligence or because of an evident affection for Nature's living world and the life of farming, Howard kept the way always open between his necessarily specialized work as a scientist and his responsibility to the Wheel of Life. His personal integrity was to honor the integrity of what he called the "one great subject": "the whole problem of health in soil, plant, animal, and man."[110] The practical effect of this upon his work was his insistence upon thinking of everything in relation to its context. In his "revolt against 'fragmentation' of knowledge," his investigation of a crop would include its "whole existence": "the plant itself in relation to the soil in which it grows, to the conditions of village agriculture under which it is cultivated, and with reference to the economic uses of the product."[111] As a researcher and teacher, he would not offer an innovation to his farmer clients that they could not afford, or that they lacked the traction power to use.

There clearly is no break or barrier between Howard's principles and his practice and the "land ethic" of his contemporary, Aldo Leopold, who wrote:

> Health is the capacity of the land for self-renewal. Conservation is our effort to understand and preserve this capacity.[112]

And:

> A thing is right when it tends to preserve the integrity, stability, and beauty of the biotic community. It is wrong when it tends otherwise.[113]

Moreover, there is no discontinuity between the ethics of Howard and Leopold and Nature's principle, given to Alan of Lille, that her good, the good of the natural world, depends upon human goodness, which is to say the human practice of the human virtues. And here I will say again that the needs of the land and the needs of the people tend always to be the same. There is always the convergence of what Nature requires for the survival of the land with what economic demand or economic adversity requires for the survival of the farmer.

From Alan's *Plaint of Nature*, and surely from the conversation of farmers and other country people before and after, it is possible to trace a living tradition of deference, respect and responsibility to Nature and her laws, carried forward by many voices speaking in agreement and in mutual help and amplification. They speak in fact with more agreement and continuity than I expected when I began this essay. And they speak, as also I now see, without so much as a glance toward moral relativism.

. . .

For many years I have known that the books by King, Smith, Howard, and Leopold, supported by other intellectually respectable books that I have not mentioned, constitute a coherent, sound, and proven argument against industrial agriculture and for an agricultural ecology and economy that, had it prevailed, would have preserved both the economic landscapes and their human communities. It is significant that all of those books, and others allied with them, were in print by the middle of the last century. Together, they might have provided a basis for the reformation of agriculture according to principles congenial to it. If that had happened, an immeasurable, and so far an illimitable, damage to the land and the people could have been prevented.

The opposite happened. All specifically agricultural and ecological standards were replaced by the specifically industrial standards of productivity, mechanical efficiency, and profitability (to agri-industrial and other corporations). Meanwhile, the criticisms and the recommendations of King, Smith, Howard, Leopold, et al., have never been addressed or answered, let alone disproved.

That they happen to have been right, by any appropriate standard, simply has not mattered to the academic and official forces of agriculture. The writings of the agrarian scientists, the validity of their science notwithstanding, have been easily ignored and overridden by wealth and power. The perfection of the industrial orthodoxy becomes clear when we remember that King, Smith, and Howard traveled the world to search out and study examples of sustainable agriculture, whereas agri-industrial scientists have traveled the world as evangelists for an agriculture unsustainable by every measure.

The truth of agrarian scientists, and their long cultural tradition, casts nevertheless a bright and exposing light upon the silliness and superficiality of the industrial economy, the industrial politicians and economists, and the industrial conservationists. Industrial politicians and economists ignore everything that can be ignored, mainly the whole outdoors. Industrial conservationists ignore everything but wilderness preservation ("Give us the 'wild' land; do as you please with the rest") and the most sensational and fashionable "environmental disasters."

.   .   .

In opposition to industrial and all other sorts and ways of subhuman consumption of the living world, the tradition of cooperation with Nature has persisted for many centuries, through many changes, sustained by right principles, the proofs of experience and eventually of science, and good sense. Its diminishment in our age has been tragic. If ever it should be lost entirely, that would be a greater "environmental disaster" than global warming. It is reassuring therefore to know that it has lasted until now, in the practice of some farmers, and in the work of some scientists. I now have in mind particularly the scientists of The Land Institute, which to me has been a source of instruction and hope for nearly half my life, and which certainly belongs in, and is in good part explained by, the cultural lineage I have been tracking.

The Land Institute was started forty years ago. It is amusing, amazing, and most surely confirmative of my argument, that when Wes Jackson laid out in his mind the order of thought that formed The Land Institute, he had never heard of Sir Albert Howard. The confirming gist of this is that Wes's ignorance of the writings of Sir Albert Howard at that time did not matter. What matters, and matters incalculably, is that Wes's formative thought developed exactly according to the pattern followed by the thinking of King, Smith, and Howard:

perception of the waste of fertility and of soil, recognition of the failure of the current standards, and the turn to Nature for a better standard.

Wes had read *Tree Crops*, which had given him the fundamental principle and pattern, which he must more and more consciously have needed. He had in himself the alertness and the sense to look about and see where he was. And like King and Howard he had grown up farming — in, as I know, an agrarian family of extraordinary intelligence and attentiveness. He grew up loving to farm. He knew, and probably long before he knew he knew, the essential truth spoken by Henry Besuden: that soil conservation "involves the heart of the man managing the land. If he loves his soil he will save it." The entire culture of husbandry is implicit in that last sentence. The practical result was, again exactly, Albert Howard's comparison of human farming to Nature's farming — or, as Wes has phrased it in many a talk, a comparison of "human cleverness" to "Nature's wisdom." Whereas Howard had looked to the woods for this, Wes, a Kansan, looked to the native prairie, a possibility that Howard himself had foreseen and approved. If you want to know what is wrong with a Kansas wheatfield, study the prairie. And then, taking his own advice, Wes conceived the long-term and ongoing project of The Land Institute: to replace the monocultures of annual grains with polycultures of grain-bearing perennials, which would have to be developed by a long endeavor of plant-breeding.

Among those who are interested, this project is well known. I want to say only two things about it: First it is radical, for it goes to the roots of the problem and to the roots of the plants. Second, there is nothing sensational about it. To Wes, having thought so far, it was obviously the next thing to be done. To any agricultural scientist whose mind had been formed as Wes's had been formed — and Wes, unique as he is, could not have been *that* unique — it ought to have been obvious. If one of only two possibilities has failed, the alternative is not far to seek.

That the need for an agriculture of perennials was obvious to nobody but Wes, and that it is still by principle unobvious to many agricultural scientists, suggests that the purpose of higher education has been to ignore or obscure the obvious.

. . .

The work of The Land Institute is as dedicated to the best interests of the land and the people as if it, rather than the present universities, had sprung from the land-grant legislation. And so the science of The Land Institute is significantly different from the industrial sciences of product development and product addiction — also from the "pure" science that seeks, with the aid of extremely costly and violent technology, the ultimate truth of the universe.

I am talking now of a science subordinate and limited, dedicated to the service of things greater than itself, as every science and art ought to be. There are some things it won't do, some dangers it won't risk. It will not, I think, commit "creative destructions," for the sake of some future good or higher truth. It is a science founded upon the traditional respect for Nature, the natural world, the farmland, and those farmers whose use of the land enacts this respect.

This old respect, really one of the highest forms of human self-respect, provides an indispensable basis, unifying and congenial, for work of all kinds. It might unify a university. In evidence, I offer the friendship that for nearly forty years has kept Wes Jackson and me talking with each other. According to the departmentalism of thought and the other fragmentations that beset us, a useful friendship or a conversation inexhaustibly interesting ought to be impossible between a scientist and a poet. That such a conversation is possible is in fact one of its most interesting subjects. Different as we necessarily are, we have much in common: an interest in the natural world, an interest in farming, an inherited agrarianism, an unresting concern about the problems of farming, of land use in general, and of rural life. Making a common interest of these subjects depends of course on speaking common English, which we can do. But that is not all.

I have heard Wes say many times that "the boundaries of causation always exceed the boundaries of consideration." The more I have thought about that statement, the more interesting it has become. The key word is "always." Mystery, the unknown, our ignorance, always will be with us, to be dealt with. The farther we extend the radius of knowledge, the larger becomes the circumference of mystery. There is, in other words, a boundary that may move somewhat, but can never be removed, between what we know and what we don't, between our human minds and the mind of Nature or the mind of God. To ignore or defy that division, wishing to be as gods, believing that the human mind is so capacious as to contain the whole universe and its whole truth, is characteristic of a kind of science that is at once romantic and industrial, ever in search of new worlds to conquer. From its work, I fear, we can expect only a continuing spillover of violence, to the world and to ourselves.

But a scientist who knows that the boundary exists and accepts, even welcomes, its existence, who knows that the boundary has a human side and elects to stay on it, is a scientist of a kind opposed to the would-be masters of the universe. A poet, too, can choose the human side of that boundary. Any artist, any scientist can so choose. Having so chosen, they can speak to one another congenially, in good faith and friendship. When we know securely the smallness of our minds relative to the immensity of our ignorance, then a certain poise and grace may become possible for us, and we can think responsibly of the circumstances in which we work, of the issues of limits and of the proprieties of scale. If we can talk of limits and of scale, we can slack off our obsession with quantities and immensities and take up the study of form: of the forms of Nature's work, of the forms by which our work might be adapted to hers. We may then become capable of the hope, that Wes and I caught years ago from our friend John Todd, for "Elegant solutions predicated upon the uniqueness of place."[114]

.   .   .

And now the long journey of my essay is ended. I have written it in order to encounter once again, and more coherently than before, the writings and the thoughts among which my own writings have formed themselves. The newest to me of the predecessors I have discussed is the oldest: Alan of Lille's *Plaint of Nature*. My reading and re-reading of that book over the last four or five years helped me to see the thread that connects the others: the books and the voices — to borrow Alan's happiest metaphor — that through many years have been in conversation in "the little town of my mind."[115]

Notes

1. C. S. Lewis, *Studies in Words*, second edition, Cambridge University Press, 1975, p. 42.
2. Alan of Lille, *The Plaint of Nature*, translation and commentary by James J. Sheridan, Pontifical Institute of Medieval Studies, 1980, p. 33.
3. Ibid., p. 67.
4. Ibid., pp. 124–25.
5. Ibid., p. 75.
6. Ibid., p. 86.
7. Ibid., p. 94.
8. Ibid., p. 99.
9. Ibid., p. 104.
10. Ibid., p. 108.
11. C. S. Lewis, *The Allegory of Love*, Oxford University Press, 1973, p. 108.
12. Alan of Lille, *The Plaint of Nature*, p. 12.
13. Ibid., p. 59.
14. Ibid., p. 46.
15. Thomas Carlyle, *Past and Present*, Everyman's Library, 1947, p. 46.
16. Thomas Merton, *The Collected Poems*, New Directions, 1977, pp. 363 and 370.
17. Geoffrey Chaucer, *The Poetical Works of Chaucer*, Cambridge Edition, F. N. Robinson, editor, Houghton Mifflin, 1933, p. 367, line 316. All further Chaucer citations are to this edition.
18. Chaucer, *The Parliament of Fowls*, p. 365, lines 176, 177.
19. Chaucer, *The Knight's Tale*, p. 54, line 2931.
20. Theodora Stanwell-Fletcher, *Driftwood Valley*, introduction by Wendell Berry, Penguin Books, 1989, p. x.
21. Chaucer, *The Nun's Priest's Tale*, p. 238, line 2828.
22. Ibid., line 2834.
23. Chaucer, *The Parliament of Fowls*, p. 369, line 499.
24. Ibid., p. 370, lines 595, 599.
25. Ibid., p. 367, line 318.
26. Chaucer, *The Parliament of Fowls*, p. 366, line 301.
27. Ibid., line 305.

28. Robert Herrick, "Corinna's Going A-Maying," lines 29–35.

29. Chaucer, *The Parliament of Fowls*, p. 367, line 319.

30. Ibid., lines 379–81.

31. Chaucer, "The Physician's Tale," p. 175, line 20.

32. Ibid., line 12.

33. Ibid., line 26.

34. Ibid., lines 13, 18.

35. *Hamlet*, III, ii, 24.

36. Edmund Spenser, *Spenser's Faerie Queene*, J. C. Smith, editor, Clarendon Press, 1909, Book II, Canto VI, stanza xxxv, lines 4–6.

37. Ibid., VII, stanza iv, lines 6–7.

38. Ibid., VII, VII, stanzas v, vi, vii, and lines 1–4, of stanza xiii.

39. Spenser, *The Faerie Queene*, VII, VII, stanza xiv, lines 1, 4–9.

40. Alan of Lille, *The Plaint of Nature*, p. 118.

41. Spenser, *The Faerie Queene*, VII, VII, iii.

42. Lewis, *The Allegory of Love*, p. 356.

43. Spenser, *The Faerie Queene*, VII, VII, xviii, lines 1–8.

44. Alan of Lille, *The Plaint of Nature*, p. 145.

45. Spenser, *The Faerie Queene*, VII, VII, stanza lix, line 9.

46. Spenser, *The Faerie Queene*, VII, VIII, stanza ii, lines 2–4.

47. Lewis, *The Allegory of Love*, p. 160, footnote.

48. William Langland, *The Vision of Piers Plowman, A Critical Edition of the B-Text*, edited by A. V. C. Schmidt, J. M. Dent and Sons, 1978, passus XI, lines 320–66, and passus XII, lines 218–28.

49. John Milton, *Comus,* stage direction, after line 658.

50. Ibid., lines 786–87.

51. Ibid., lines 710–14, 720–24.

52. Ibid., line 246.

53. Ibid., lines 765–73.

54. Pope, "Epistle to Burlington," lines 109, 108.

55. Ibid., line 43.

56. Ibid., lines 50, 57.

57. Ibid., line 167.

58. Ibid., lines 173–76.

59. Ibid., lines 179–80.

60. William Wordsworth, "Lines Composed a Few Miles Above Tintern Abbey," lines 25–26, 39–40, 52–53.

61. Ibid., lines 47–49.

62. Ibid., lines 94–97.

63. Ibid., lines 108–11.

64. Ibid., lines 122–25.

65. Ibid., line 131.

66. Matthew 5:45.

67. Wordsworth, "Tintern Abbey," line 152.

68. Ibid., lines 120–22.

69. Ibid., lines 46–48.

70. Ibid., lines 189, 194–98.

71. Ibid., line 211.

72. Ibid., lines 249–50.

73. Ibid., lines 252–55.

74. Ibid., line 433.

75. Ibid., lines 442–47.

76. Ibid, line 475.

77. Hayden Carruth, "Marshall Washer," in *Collected Shorter Poems, 1946–1991*, Copper Canyon Press, 1992, pp. 171.

78. Ibid., p. 175.

79. Lester Flatt and Earl Scruggs, "The Homestead on the Farm," in *Songs of the Famous Carter Family, Featuring Mother Maybelle Carter and the Foggy Mountain Boys,* CD, Columbia Records, n.d..

80. Ezra Pound, *The Cantos of Ezra Pound*, Faber & Faber, 1964, Canto LI, p. 261.

81. Ibid., Canto XCIX, p. 734.

82. Ibid., Canto LIII, p. 278.

83. Ibid., Canto LXXXI, p. 556.

84. Gary Snyder, "Water Music II," *No Nature*, Pantheon, 1992, p. 196.

85. Jacques Maritain, *Art and Scholasticism with Other Essays*, translated by J. F. Scanlan, Charles Scribner's Sons, 1947, p. 52.

86. G. C. Coulton, *Medieval Panorama*, Meridian Books, 1955, pp. 103–4.

87. Ibid., p. 240.

88. *Beef Producer*, Oct. 2015, p. 7.

89. Mr. Besuden's story and his several remarks come from my essay, "A Talent for Necessity," *The Gift of Good Land*, North Point Press, 1981, pp. 227–37.

90. F. H. King, *Farmers of Forty Centuries*, Rodale Press, 1911 (reprinted, n.d.) p. 1.

91. Ibid.

92. Ibid.

93. Ibid., p. 3.

94. Ibid., p. 13.

95. Ibid., p. 234.

96. J. Russell Smith, *Tree Crops*, Harcourt, Brace and Company, 1929, p. 4.

97. Ibid., p. 3.

98. Ibid., p. 11.

99. Ibid., p. 16.

100. Ibid., p. 259.

101. Ibid., p. 260.

102. Sir Albert Howard, *An Agricultural Testament*, Oxford University Press, 1940, p. 1.

103. Ibid., p. ix.

104. Ibid., p. 4.

105. Ibid, p. ix.

106. Louise E. Howard, *Sir Albert Howard in India*, The Rodale Press, 1954, p. 221.

107. Sir Albert Howard, *The Soil and Health*, Schocken Books, [1947] 1972, p. 18.

108. Ibid., p. 63.

109. L. E. Howard, *Sir Albert Howard in India*, p. 20.

110. Howard, *The Soil and Health*, p. 11.

111. L. E. Howard, *Sir Albert Howard in India*, p. 42.

112. Aldo Leopold, *A Sand County Almanac*, Oxford University Press, 1966, p. 236.

113. Ibid., p. 240.

114. John Todd, "Tomorrow Is Our Permanent Address," in *The Book of the New Alchemists*, edited by Nancy Jack Todd, E. P. Dutton, 1977, p. 116.

115. Alan of Lille, *Plaint*, p. 193.

Acknowledgments

In the essay that is Part III of this book I acknowledge more of my debts than in anything I have written before. But I am obliged also for helps directly involved in the making of this book, and I want to mention them here.

To the four couples named on the dedication page, to their households and families, I owe thanks for decades of hospitality and conversation that have been indispensible to my work, and to the life that Tanya and I and our family have made.

This book has a large debt to Christopher Bamford, who gave me my first understanding of the importance of Alan of Lille's *Plaint of Nature* and sent me translations.

I thank also John Lukacs, Marc Hudson, and Jim Powell who read the manuscript of "The Presence of Nature in the Natural World" and gave me useful advice;

Julie Wrinn, who copyedited the essay, improving it very much by her corrections and suggestions, and thereby improving my own sense of what was needed;

David Charlton and Michele Guthrie, who patiently and kindly made this book electronically transmissible;

Tanya Berry, who typed and retyped, read and reread the various parts of this book, giving me all the while the benefit of her good sense.

I am indebted, moreover, to Tanya and our children, not only for generous companionship, but also for their thoughts and their ways of thinking.

The making of this book has extraordinarily burdened the patience of Jack Shoemaker of Counterpoint, my friend, editor, and collaborator for forty years. For patience and much else, I thank him. I thank also my other friends at Counterpoint.

For many years, and again now, my books have been improved by the designs of David Bullen. I give him my thanks, old and new.

It is only appropriate that in the pages of this particular book I should remember and thank my teachers, Arthur K. Moore and Thomas B. Stroup, who helped me learn to read Chaucer and Milton, and whose sense of the importance of those writers, and of writing, has kept with me more than sixty years.

Finally I thank the editors of *The Sewanee Review* for publishing several of the poems of *Sabbaths 2014*.